THE COMMON GOOD IN THE 21st CENTURY

A Convoco Edition

CORINNE MICHAELA FLICK (ED.)

Convoco! Editions

Convoco Foundation
Brienner Strasse 28
D – 80333 Munich
www.convoco.co.uk

British Library Cataloguing-in-Publication data: a catalogue
record for this book is available from the British Library.

Edited by Dr. Corinne Michaela Flick
Translated from German by Philippa Hurd
Layout and typesetting by Jill Sawyer Phypers
Printed and bound in Great Britain by Clays Ltd., St Ives plc

ISBN: 978-0-9931953-6-5

Previously published Convoco titles:

Authority in Transformation (2017)

Power and its Paradoxes (2016)

To Do or Not To Do—Inaction as a Form of Action (2015)

Dealing with Downturns: Strategies in Uncertain Times (2014)

Collective Law-Breaking—A Threat to Liberty (2013)

Who Owns the World's Knowledge? (2012)

**Can't Pay, Won't Pay? Sovereign Debt and the Challenge of
Growth in Europe (2011)**

It is one of my principles that one must work for the common good, and to the extent that one has contributed towards it, to that same extent will one feel contented.

—*Gottfried Wilhelm Leibniz (1646–1716)*

CONTENTS

INTRODUCTION

Dear Friends of Convoco,

Recently, it has looked as if the common good might be disappearing as a guiding principle of our society.

In a world where nationalism is becoming more dominant (think of Donald Trump's "America First" agenda), protectionism is pursued ("une Europe qui protège," as announced by France's President Macron), and society too is disintegrating into an increasing number of parts, the idea that we need to think about the common good seems to be progressively weakening. More and more frequently we are confronted with the charge that in the Western world, in particular, governments as well as economic and intellectual elites are moving away from the people, who are the real sovereign power.

As is widely agreed, the principle of the common good is essential for our society's cohesiveness, as a focus on it can bring the individual parts of society closer together again.

"Common good" in English, *bonum commune* in Latin, or *Gemeinwohl* in German: they all mean the general well-being of *one* society. This assumes a community that primarily places the common interest—that is, the interests of the community as a whole—above the individual interest. To be motivated to do this, it is important that the individual feels a sense of belonging to the community itself.[1]

Today's world consists of communities established by diverse groups of people, beginning with the family, via the state, to global organizations. We have an increased sense of responsibility to the members of the communities to which we feel we belong. But we also have moral obligations—or so the essays in this volume suggest—towards people outside these communities.

In most cases, our modern political communities are defined by territorial thinking—the common good of the *polis* or the nation-state. Increasingly, however, the concept of the common good is acquiring a global, post-national dimension.[2] Ultimately, the *bonum commune* cannot be separated from the universal idea of the good. Thus the concept of the common good, in the end, focuses on humanity as a whole.

Today, it is coming to be acknowledged that a specific common good exists at a global level—and there are also self-interested reasons for upholding this. For example, in the case of issues such as climate or health, it is vital to think and cooperate transnationally. We must not ignore our obligation to act as a global community of states. We need to understand which problems are to be managed better in Europe or internationally, rather than unilaterally.

According to Aristotle's famous formulation, a human being is a *zoon politikon*, a "political being", who finds his or her true nature in the communitarian life of the *polis*. This has far-reaching consequences. The kind of person a human being becomes is dependent on the social, cultural, and institutional circumstances of their life, not only on their personal success and prosperity. In this, we can see how important the common good, the *bonum commune*, is for the individual. The common good should be seen as the basic requirement for human personal development, and it should serve this. It is not an end in itself: the individual can make use of the common good as a social resource on which they can rely.

Essentially, the common good describes the relationship between the individual and society. This goes back not only to Aristotle, but also to Plato. Both philosophers were agreed that the well-being of the individual and of society are connected, but they came up with different approaches.

According to Plato, the well-being of the community is an objective, normative value system that is common to the citizens of a state. The *bonum commune* should be understood in this sense as an ethical value, a principle that serves to direct behavior. The Constitution of the United States and Germany's Basic Law are examples of such normative value systems. For Plato, the realization of justice was an element of the common good. According to this understanding, those in power must set aside their personal interests, and individual members of society must set aside their individual interests in favor of the well-being of all. Both must subordinate themselves to the good and happy life of all citizens. For Plato, the expression of justice was general legislation and equality before the law.

The other understanding of the common good is empirical. It goes back to Aristotle's idea that the common good is a product of social systems and institutions that work together in such a way that all people profit from it. Freedom and autonomy can be realized here through the active participation of individuals.

This understanding can be seen, for example, in the English legal system of "common law."

A functioning, modern common good is expected to both serve as a guiding principle and offer practical processes through which society can flourish. It is important to look at both approaches afresh, and to place the common good once again at the heart of our thinking, as today it seems as if what we once regarded as "one society" is no longer aware of its common values. The "we" is in the process of being lost.

One guarantee of the common good as a social resource is the state. It is the only entity that can legitimately enforce the common good. By being a citizen, the individual sacrifices a part of their freedom to the state. Compensation for this loss of freedom resides in the individual being able to shape better their individual well-being on the basis of the common good. In this context, the question arises of who defines the common good. In parliamentary democracies, the common good is decided through binding procedures. It is legislators who decide—that is, ultimately, the majority in a democracy; but of course alongside the procedural majority decision there is also a debate within society that defines what the common good is. This is where public opinion contributes, as well as scientific, ethical, and religious insights. As a normative fundamental structure, the constitution alone does not determine what the common good is, but rather it provides the basis for its agreement and ratification.[3]

Our interpretation of the common good is also expressed in the concept of the social market economy through the principles of the welfare state and the rule of law. The three fundamental principles of personality, solidarity, and subsidiarity characterize the social market economy.[4] This means that, in the case of personal fulfillment, responsibility for the community, namely solidarity, appears alongside personal responsibility. Here, it should also be noted that the individual's self-help is invoked first, before help from the community. This is the meaning of subsidiarity.

It is important that society maintains its public spirit: that is, its engagement in the well-being of the community. After all, it was through the founding of communities that men became *one* political power. This "horizontal" or lateral consciousness emerged first in the city republics of antiquity and was reaffirmed in the Renaissance, and it forms the basis of our social systems even today. We should give our society a direction, and take the common good as its focal point. This is of particular relevance in light of the technological developments that are approaching in this century. It is clear, for example, that major changes in the labor market of the future will come about as a result of artificial intelligence and increasing digitalization. What these changes will look like remains to be seen. It is likely that work will no longer be a determining factor as an individual's mark of identity in the way it once was. Humankind has reached the place in evolution it currently occupies thanks to its desire, and not just its ability, to cooperate. The ability to build communities using the division of labor and complex strategies has established the position of humankind as the "pinnacle of creation." The advance of artificial intelligence, combined with algorithms and big data, means humankind is now in danger of losing this position. We should acknowledge the central role of community and its relevance for the 21st century.

Corinne Michaela Flick, January 2018

Notes

1. A study of taxation has shown that the sense of belonging operates in proportion to the willingness to pay taxes. See Benny Geys and Kai A. Konrad, "Patriotism and Taxation", *Working Paper of the Max Planck Institute for Tax Law and Public Finance*, no. 2016-11 (November 11, 2016).

2. Bernd Ladwig, "Liberales Gemeinwohl—Von den Schwierigkeiten einer Idee und ihrem Verhältnis zur Gerechtigkeit" in *Gemeinwohl und Gemeinsinn. Zwischen Normativität und Faktizität*, vol. IV, ed. by Herfried Münkler and Harald Bluhm (Berlin: Akademie Verlag, 2002), p. 93.

3. See also Udo Di Fabio, "The Common Good of the Global Society," in the present volume, pp. 17–37.

4. Timo Meynhardt and Alexander Schumann, "Aufgeschoben, nicht aufgehoben" in *Berliner Republik*, vol. 4 (2009).

THESES

TIMO MEYNHARDT

The common good is a necessary fiction—a focus, as it were, on the greater whole, which only then takes shape, and which as a result in turn creates a system. To evoke an image, the idea of the common good is like the function of a polestar that can never be reached but can always indicate a direction. In light of today's economic and social challenges, we might even say that if complexity is the challenge, the common good is the answer.

UDO DI FABIO

In debates about the common good it is striking that almost all participants believe that it is clear what the common good is, and how one might preserve or promote it. In reality, almost everything in this context is contingent: that means we could almost always make a different choice and state the exact opposite.

BAZON BROCK

Today, the common good is that which gives members of a community the freedom to develop their individuality, or constitutionally enables the community to live with a multiplicity of religious convictions without the competition that results in obliteration. This means that the common good applies to the development, education, and encouragement of individuality.

WOLFGANG SCHÖN

As unconvincing as it may be to want to realize the "global common good" on all political fronts, a general re-nationalization of interests is equally incapable of solving the world's real problems. It seems right to focus on different political reference systems depending on the topic. The citizen will have to be prepared to think and act as a German/Frenchman/Englishman, a European, or a global citizen depending on the topic—otherwise their thinking will be too small or too big.

STEFAN KORIOTH

Why, even in 2017, do our notions of justice and the common good concern themselves so stubbornly (and thus perhaps also justifiably) with the system of groups living at the same time and in the same place, from the family to the nation, using the juxtapositions of inclusion and exclusion, today and tomorrow, inward-looking altruism and outward-looking egotism?

RUDOLF MELLINGHOFF

The legislature takes account of the interests of the common good in tax law in a variety of ways. Public-benefit law is particularly significant in this respect. Beyond this, the Basic Law also permits the legislature to deviate from imposing taxation based on economic resources if the legislature wants to advance the interests of the common good by doing so. This proves that tax law is an important component of a policy that focuses on general welfare.

JENS SPAHN

The common good is expressed in nothing more than the figures and finances of a federal budget—that is as true today as it will be in 2030.

CHRISTOPH G. PAULUS

Even if everyone has a vague, rather unclear notion of what the common good means concretely—even in the 21st century—it is far easier to identify things that are detrimental to the common good and run counter to it. One of these things is the burden of debt on public finances, not only in Germany but, appallingly, almost across the entire world.

ROLAND BERGER

Companies can best contribute to increasing the common good if they focus on their core tasks: creating value for the individual and the community. I am convinced that in our market-based economic system rooted in the division of labor, companies fundamentally contribute most to the common good when they are fully committed to their business.

KAI A. KONRAD

The entrepreneur who wants only to maximize their profit thus contributes in the maximum way possible to the prosperity of society precisely through the one-sided focus of their activity on their own profit. If politics creates the right regulatory framework, the objectives of the entrepreneur's one-sided focus on profit and the general prosperity of society will not be in conflict.

STEFAN OSCHMANN

Health is part of the common good. But for innovation to thrive, we depend on health care products and services being developed by private players. And we need the private sector to lean in to work towards equitable access to health.

CARL BENEDIKT FREY

On average, automation has always benefited society, but sometimes at the expense of large parts of the workforce whose jobs have disappeared. It is up to society to make computerization a common good by making sure that its benefits are widely shared. It is not a common good *per se*.

JÖRG ROCHOLL

The common good will not benefit if people who are not thought capable of working with new technologies are encouraged to do nothing as a result of an unconditional basic income. Extensive efforts to improve educational opportunities will be more important for the common good in the long term, and will enable participation in economic progress and social exchange.

HITO STEYERL

Maybe future AIs will be conscious or maybe not. The point is that there are so many existing phenomena already, that we need to deal with those that are being caused by the by-products of all these technological developments. If you're just always in awe of a coming either benevolent or obnoxious singularity, then you will fail to recognise that our societies now are already being restructured in a way that enables post-fascism, nativism, populism, unemployment, and all of these things.

HANS ULRICH OBRIST

When considering the dangers of artificial intelligence, the critical thinking practiced by artists is helpful. As AI's algorithms are made visible through artificial images in new ways, artists' critical visual knowledge and expertise can be harnessed. Many of the key questions concerning AI are philosophical in nature, and can therefore only be answered from an holistic point of view.

CLEMENS FUEST

Awareness of the importance of the common good and of threats to it is a good basis on which to protect the common good in the future as well.

CORINNE M. FLICK

It is important that society maintains its public spirit: that is, its engagement in the well-being of the community. We should give our society a direction, and take the common good as its focal point. This is of particular relevance in light of the technological developments that are approaching in this century. The ability to build communities has established the position of humankind as the "pinnacle of creation." This ability will also continue to be the best way of protecting people from the excessive power of artificial intelligence, algorithms, and big data.

CHAPTER 1

THE COMMON GOOD OF THE GLOBAL SOCIETY

UDO DI FABIO

1. Debate about the common good, the quest for the *bonum commune*,[1] operates within a formula of political theories of justice.[2] This is based on the belief that an act of cognition can determine what the fundamental aims and purposes of a political society are and should be. Today, modern theories of democracy mainly assume that such a substantive definition of the common good cannot possibly aspire to the truth, as the individualization and plurality of a free society already present obstacles to this.[3] And so, the theories claim, the common good is *proceduralized*, which

means that it is ultimately that upon which the majority has decided via a formal procedure. If the German Bundestag decides that nuclear energy production is beneficial, the growth of nuclear energy is in accordance with the common good. If the Bundestag later decides that only the withdrawal from and abandonment of nuclear energy corresponds to the common good, then this is now the new common good. In this vein, the common good is what a parliament or a European council decides is the law, in either case via a formally established procedure.[4] As a concept in the generation of political theory, however, the common good is thus an empty phrase—basically deprived of its self-willed, regulating power.

2. As is so often the case, the reality is somewhat more complicated than it appears in this distinction between a substantive and a procedural understanding of the common good. In political debate, decisions are being justified more and more using the notion of the common good, and from this perspective they are then presented as almost without alternative. There is a *raison d'état* that highlights the crux of a political community's understanding of the common good. If the preservation of natural resources is written in the constitution,[5] this provides a kind of state objective that

aspires to formulate an element of the common good in a way that goes beyond parliament's substantively vague freedom to decide. State objectives and constitutional obligations should make material notions of the common good binding for the democratic majority as well. The courts that are called upon to interpret these obligations towards the common good ultimately make the decisions. Constitutional obligations, such as the goal of the welfare state or a constitutional decision in favor of European integration and international cooperation, may play a relatively minor role in the everyday implementation of the constitution, but they do form guidelines and benchmarks for the workings of the political system. Consequently, in the principle of democratic majority as part of the mechanics of the constitution, we find strong evidence pointing to the procedural variant of our understanding of the common good and, in terms of state goals themselves, a measure of substantive proportionality as well.

3. In the process of political policy-making, constitutional law is not the only place where a substantive definition of the common good is at issue. Political philosophy or constitutional theory also make scholarly contributions here. Even more important is the formation of public opinion as it reflects an everyday

notion of political morality and ideas of public or individual justice respectively. Public opinion considers itself free to modify and change the amount of attention paid to and views on the fundamental goals of a state or a political regime. Between academia and political policy-making there often exist smooth transitions as well as strategic attempts to push the idea of what the guiding principle of the aim of the common good is in a desired direction that is appropriate in each case. Ergo: the common good is not an objective fact but rather a social construct which differed in the time of Pericles from what it was in the time of the Roman emperor Caligula or in the time of Charlemagne, and which today is different in Iran or China from what it is in Sweden or Chad.

Those who are not happy with these postmodern, constructivist findings can rest assured that there is an objective seam of the common good at least in the most extreme existential conditions of a social or political community. It is clearly to the detriment of the common good if the natural, social, economic, or political resources of a community are destroyed. This would shift the question to what the crucial conditions of existence are, whether and how they are put at risk, and how the situation could be remedied—that is ultimately a debate concerning decisions about selection and truth-apt questions. For example, today climate change is regarded as self-harm caused by the human race, and to this extent it is formulated in a global perspective as a condition of existence and remedies sought at global climate conferences. But here too, by definition, there is no determining certainty, because the US President would either deny the dangers of climate change or define it as not existentially threatening to the American people, and thus he would give a different meaning to both the factual basis and the benchmark for considerations of the common good. A right-wing populist would perhaps see a people's livelihood threatened by migration, while at NATO headquarters an effective increase in armaments might be seen as a decisive measure in guaranteeing peace, and thus as a condition of existence for free Western societies and an overriding concern when it comes to the common good. The foreign policy community might argue about whether it serves the common good or the European Union to be independent of Russian gas imports, or whether—conversely—it serves the peace brought about through trade and commerce to open up Russia's business prospects with the West and expand these prospects.

The fact remains that in debates about the common good it is striking that almost all participants believe that it is clear what the common good is, and how one might preserve or promote it. In reality, almost everything in this context is contingent: that means we could almost always make a different choice and state the exact opposite. For this reason, it is not just academics but critical citizens as well who are suspicious when politicians or activists talk about the common good.

4. A particular need for clarification regarding the common good has arisen through the process of globalization. By globalization, most parties understand the increase in economic, scientific, or communications traffic across national borders. A globalized economy is one that not only sees the whole world as a sales outlet but also organizes the entire goods production process and supply of services across the globe based on the division of labor. Digging a little deeper, sociology talks about "global society,"[6] as the traditional idea of society linked to national culture is losing its foundations, and international relations cannot simply be understood as external relations in a social system comprising individual nations. Every Internet user, every consumer, every transnational company, and every political regime that thinks in geopolitical terms ultimately operates at the level of the global society

and not at the level of the nation-state (which is not just or no longer seen as significant).

This global society perspective makes the definition of the common good even more difficult; it makes the contingency common to public discourse very variable. Without the practical reality of a world state, one cannot simply refer back to a procedural formula, as is usual within democracies, and political camps that espouse contrasting notions of the common good cannot be created.[7] This is true regardless of the fact that the UN Security Council, the OECD, or the WTO system, as well as the increasing number of commitments that are constitutionally based, for example on climate protection, have created significant platforms for transnational government, internationalized community-building, and thus also for forms of legal concretization of political guidelines and goals, that are of transnational common good. But this space of transnational, political hegemony has in no respect attained the durability and stability of the classic, modern state, albeit it may appear to have done so to some extent in the EU, though here too cohesion and the fundamental establishment of goals remain precarious and contentious.

In this, the old constructive conflict within recent concepts of the state remains unchanged, and is even exacerbated in some ways: the idea of territorially limited governance had made it possible to personalize political power, initially in the sovereignty of the aristocracy, then in the democratic principle of the sovereignty of the people. National borders interrupt any notions of interdependence and make the notion of a space of collective development plausible. In this case, in a liberal interpretation, the common good can be seen in the collective guarantee of individual freedom and the individual pursuit of happiness or—in a more collectivistic way bordering on nationalism— as a people's aspiration to self-realization. The disastrous, excessive nationalism in Europe of the pre-1914 period up to the end of World War II was focused on the national common good and thus destroyed any opportunities for a European and international peace. But regardless of one-sidedness and radicalization it remains the case that:

> Ever since its origins in the works of Jean Bodin and Giovanni Botero, the principle of the state has been in conflict with the universalist traditions of Christianity and later of the liberal Enlightenment, as demonstrated by the twin drafting of human rights and civil rights as included in France's revolutionary constitutions.[8]

It depends on the *point of reference*. It depends what one wants to associate the common good with:

with oneself, with one's own family, with Bavaria, Catalonia, Italy, Germany, or Europe, or the world and every single person living in it. The fundamental rights in Germany's Basic Law as they address rightful claimants distinguish between German citizens on the one hand, and on the other people in general who fall within the sphere of influence of German state power. Accordingly, a *rational concept of the common good* must identify and explain its points of reference, and how various points of reference are brought together in a meaningful context, so that one is not played off against the other in a destructive way. Moreover, a concept of the common good is only rational if it respects and satisfies the conditions of freedom and functioning of the various actors involved. The consistent military enforcement of human rights could directly result in a major war that would mean the end of civilization. If a consistent climate policy cannot be achieved through democracies, should we consider a dictatorship, for example? However, based on all previous experience, judged on its merits and above all according to our normative understanding of freedom, isn't a dictatorship inimical to the common good right from the outset?

On closer examination, discussion of the common good turns out to be just as contingent and indeed arbitrary as the thesis concerning justice: things become more vague the larger the social and political entities to which they refer. In such cases, a global common good is not a concept that is rationally manageable. In any case, there are too many points of reference and common good benefits to be offset and juxtaposed, as well as facts and norms to be reconciled, for us to grasp the concept directly, in a way that is not mediated by organizations, and for the common good to be valid as an argument. What can be clear and concise in the small or isolated and autonomous entities of a family or a rural community becomes an *arbitrary* argument at the level of global society. To focus and rationalize the common good argument we need an invariable, normative point of reference that allows for differentiations and judgments. The modern form of society in the West has prioritized the principle of freedom, construed as individual freedom of development and self-determination, but it has mapped essential, arbitrary, or traditional communities onto the issue of the common good for the purposes of constructive tension.[9]

The reconciliation of the individual with the communitarian perspective, as well as the particular with the universal point of view, results in a state legal system that shows minimal consistency, that respects fundamental civil liberties as a constitutional democracy, and at the same time works towards the principles of peace and freedom both internally and externally.[10] This is the idea of the open constitutional state that is inclusive and cooperative.[11]

Thus far, the concordance of individual and universal human rights has succeeded particularly well in the idea of the open constitutional state, but seems to have demonstrated its structural limits when openness and inclusivity lead gradually to an undermining of the possibility of autonomous self-determination.[12] Frequently, the logical, functional system of world trade with the dismantling of trade barriers and the promotion of reasonably fair competition is the lowest common denominator on which the nations of the world with their sometimes very conflicting interests can agree—alongside general peace proposals and the de-escalation of conflict.

Equally, the history of European integration follows the model of a functional consensus and is built around the four basic economic freedoms within the concept of the internal market.[13] In this situation, however, certain more deeply rooted themes such as social justice or religiously meaningful life remain banished from the repertoire of the common good in global society, as here the differences and incompatibilities are too great. In the recent past, we can see that national, political spaces are not losing their function as quickly as the architects of the post-national constellation predicted. Emotionally, culturally, and linguistically, basic ideas of social justice and social cohesion remain linked to primary living environments and national or regional alliances. The search for a dominant culture[14] in immigrant societies or for the identity of nations, of Europe, of EU Members, or of Western Europe, is a pointer in this direction.

5. Against this backdrop, it is again extremely important to expose the core of the West's social model based on freedom, particularly in its universal aspirations, and to question the *bonum commune* of global society beyond mainstream political formations. In 1776, the American Declaration of Independence established its notion of the common good in opposition to the British Crown: "We hold these truths to be self-evident, that all men are created equal, that they are endowed by their Creator with certain unalienable rights, that among these are Life, Liberty and the pursuit of Happiness." Behind this lies the belief that there is not only proceduralization for deciding the common good in parliament, but also proceduralization in the mind of every individual who makes

decisions about themselves, about their life, about their future, about what their road to happiness is. This imperative towards individual freedom is not the last word in the definition of the common good, but the first—the point of departure for any logical deduction of the goals of the common good on the basis of a society's fundamental normative order. Based on the imperative of personal freedom and individual dignity, every political system has to organize itself in such a way that the freely developing individual is the focus—with their dignity, their right to respect, and their ability to determine their own destiny. For freedom to succeed in this light we need stronger institutional provisions, the preservation and maintenance of rationally organized functional systems, and considerable efforts to educate people, for their physical and spiritual livelihoods, that is above all for socio-cultural sustainability.[15]

The state, any other political community, and their organizations are the guarantors of a peaceful, stable, and fair system of development, which allows every person of good will to determine their life and to find their place in society. Seen in this way, the common good is not necessarily to be found where politics makes concrete, material promises to people, as such promises would first of all have to prove their suitability for the common good in terms of a system of development that was individual but also compatible with global society. Every action that is justified politically using arguments about justice must subject itself to a sustainability test in light of the supporting systems of institutions. For example, anyone who makes the scandalously high youth unemployment in some EU Member States into an issue of justice, and then sees the solution to this problem in direct subsidies and financial claims for compensation, must accept critical questions about what such state-induced transfers or transfers under national responsibility actually achieve, and above all what costs and side-effects they produce. It is possible that youth unemployment can only be combatted sustainably—if it is not merely to be a flash-in-the-pan—if school education and vocational training is designed with a more practical bent, if the conditions for economic development in some countries turn out more favorably than hitherto, and the motivation to upward social mobility is sufficiently present in the young people as well.

As another example, those who believe that an unconditional basic income is a requirement of social justice and prudence, or even an aspiration arising from human dignity, should consider what consequences are entailed by such an apparently radically simple solution to all tricky problems in activating labor market policy. For, if it is true that most people are only included in mainstream society via the constraints and demands of work, then (except for the surely more aspirational experience of the elites) a huge void might appear in the wider community who earn a reasonable living, and the dialectic of practical self-development, which always finds its real existence in a combination of freedom and constraint, might be replaced by the paternalism of a publicly organized provision of bread and circuses. Here too we can see that the definition of the common good, like arguments about justice, depends completely on empirical facts on the one hand and on the selection of normative principles on the other. It is necessary to decide transparently on what is brought about by which action, and whether means and ends lead to a result that is actually desired by individuals or by their legitimated collectives, and corresponds to their fundamental order of values.

6. Similarly, the Internet or the ethics of artificial intelligence need transparent debates about the common good. On the one hand, the idea of first-generation Internet activists, who saw the emergence of a "digital *agora*" that would establish a space for political opinions in global society and thus make the classical nations of the world completely dispensable,

has clearly not been fulfilled. But on the other hand, a communicative cross-border interdependence does exist, which, however, does not reach the system and performance levels of traditional, national public life. The digital world today is all about exploring the limits to freedom of expression, but also about critically examining the measures already introduced to combat hatred and disinformation.[16] At the same time, it is a question of preserving a fair, competitive system and proprietary rights, which should set limits with regard to the value-added models of the Internet giants.[17] Here too, the definition of the public common good on the Internet or when dealing with automated systems, for example in the case of autonomous driving,[18] cannot be entrusted solely to the contingencies of a political or economic discourse that is otherwise beneficial. Rather, it requires deep reflection based on a free modern society's idea of man and its worldview.

7. In other words, while on the one hand it is impossible not to engage in more serious debate about the substantive definition of the common good once again, on the other hand in so doing we also need to proceed in a more ambitious and informed way than before. Self-assertion, that is the development and dissemination of free, democratic systems, is the precondition of

a global, sustainable realization of the common good. Without functioning constitutional states, there is no prospect of respecting human rights and realizing the goals of global humankind. Democracies based on a market economy must stabilize their internal functionality and act at an international level with vision and sound judgment. Who can control what? Who can decide on what? Who is legally able to do what? Who can guarantee peace where and when and by what means? Questions about the global common good are first and foremost practical questions that must be advanced by negotiation within states themselves, in the institutional system of the United Nations, and in supranational and international organizations. At the same time, the socio-cultural sustainability of political objectives must be taken into account more substantially than in the past, so that the balance between global developmental goals and the conditions for preserving political communities of solidarity is not lost. International NGOs are important correctives[19] and not the dark powers imagined to be bogeymen by conspiracy theory nationalists. But, equally, they are not the indisputable authorities on the common good which, with excessive moral certainty at every conference, demonstrate to democracies and states their wretched particularism with regard to their own selective, humanitarian goals.

Assuming political responsibility means drilling through those hard boards that Max Weber once talked about, balancing conflicting interests, building bridges between governance and informing the voters, and, with the expectation of acceptance, mobilizing the resources we need to promote a humane and sustainable global order of peace and development.

Notes

1. For Thomas Aquinas the *bonum commune* is a "pivotal concept in his legal and political philosophy." Ernst-Wolfgang Böckenförde, "Klassische Gemeinwohlvorstellungen bei Klassikern der Rechts- und Staatsphilosophie" in *Gemeinwohl und Gemeinsinn im Recht. Konkretisierung und Realisierung öffentlicher Interessen,* ed. by Herfried Münkler and Karsten Fischer (Berlin: Akademie Verlag, 2002), p. 43 (51).

2. On the idea of political justice, see Otfried Höffe, *Politische Gerechtigkeit. Grundlegung einer kritischen Philosophie von Recht und Staat* (Frankfurt am Main: Suhrkamp, 1989), p. 41 ff.

3. On this, see Dieter Grimm, "Ursprung und Wandel der Verfassung" in *Handbuch des Staatsrechts,* vol. I, ed. by Josef Isensee and Paul Kirchhof, Historische Grundlagen, 3rd edn. (Heidelberg: C.F. Müller, 2003), para. 1, note 24.

4. Niklas Luhmann, *Legitimation durch Verfahren,* 10th edn. (Frankfurt am Main: Suhrkamp, 1983). If we take the procedural perspective of a definition of the common

good seriously, a further step could depend on aligning the constitution and management, for example of administrative procedures, with this function of concretizing of the common good. On this, see Gunnar Folke Schuppert, "Gemeinwohldefinition im kooperativen Staat" in Münkler and Fischer, op. cit., p. 67 (79 ff.).

5. Art. 20a Basic Law, incorporated by the law of October 27, 1994.

6. See Rudolf Stichweh, *Die Weltgesellschaft,* (Frankfurt am Main: Suhrkamp, 2000); Mathias Albert and Rudolf Stichweh (eds.), *Weltstaat und Weltstaatlichkeit. Beobachtungen globaler politischer Strukturbildung,* (Wiesbaden: VS Verlag für Sozialwissenschaften, 2007); Bettina Heintz, Richard Münch, and Hartmann Tyrell (eds.), *Weltgesellschaft. Theoretische Zugänge und empirische Problemlagen, Zeitschrift für Soziologie,* special issue (Stuttgart: Lucius & Lucius, 2005).

7. An example would be the dispute over the Brandt government's policy towards Eastern Europe at the start of the 1970s. It was openly discussed whether reunification would be advanced (as the government claimed) by the so-called *Ostverträge* [social, political, and economic treaties agreed between West Germany and certain Soviet bloc countries], or jeopardized (as the opposition maintained). Lurking beneath this was the question of whether the Reunification Clause in Germany's Basic Law was in the interest of the common good at all, or not, or whether it would in any case have to yield to the overriding interest of the common good in peacekeeping operations. BVerfGE 36, 1 (17); 77, 137 (149 ff.).

8. Franz-Xaver Kaufmann, "Sozialstaatliche Solidarität und Umverteilung im internationalen Wettbewerb" in *Transnationale Solidarität. Chancen und Grenzen,* ed. by Jens Beckert, et al. (Frankfurt am Main: Campus Verlag, 2004), p. 51 (58). See also Udo Di Fabio, *Schwankender Westen* (Munich: C.H. Beck, 2015), p. 139 ff.

9. On the context in the history of ideas see Ernst-Wolfgang Böckenförde, "Klassische Gemeinwohlvorstellungen bei Klassikern der Rechts-und Staatsphilosophie" in Münkler and Fischer, op. cit., p. 43 (54 ff.).

10. In the Basic Law, the focus on the common good and the development of an international framework for peace is made clear in the Preamble and in Art. 1 (2), Art. 23 (1) first sentence, and Art. 24 (1).

11. Udo Di Fabio, *Der Verfassungsstaat in der Weltgesellschaft* (Tübingen: Mohr Siebeck, 2001).

12. Udo Di Fabio, "Verfassungsrechtliche Entwicklungsperspektiven für die Wirtschafts- und Währungsunion" in *Von Ursprung und Ziel der Europäischen Union*, ed. by Gregor Kirchhof, Hanno Kube, and Reiner Schmidt (Tübingen: Mohr Siebeck, 2017), p. 45 (47 ff.).

13. Art. 3 (3) of the Treaty on European Union (TEU) highlights the real core of Europe's functional union, covered by the goals of peace and prosperity named in Art. 1 (3) TEU and supplemented by the single judicial area referred to in Art. 2 of the regulation.

14. Samuel Skipper, *The Politics of Immigration. Is Germany Moving towards a Multicultural Society?* (Hamburg: Anchor Academic Publishing, 2017), p. 23 ff.

15. For more details, see Di Fabio, *Schwankender Westen*, op. cit., p. 27 ff, p. 137 ff.

16. Karl-Eberhard Hain, Tobias Brings-Wiesen, and Frederik Ferreau, "Regulierung sozialer Netzwerke Revisited" in *K&R*, vol. 7/8 (2017), p. 433 ff.

17. Udo Di Fabio, *Grundrechtsgeltung in digitalen Systemen* (Munich: C.H. Beck, 2016), p. 11 ff.

18. For example, see the June 2017 report by the Ethics Commission on Automated Driving set up by Germany's Transport Minister, https://www.bmvi.de/SharedDocs/

DE/Publikationen/G/bericht-der-ethik-kommission.pdf?__
blob=publicationFile (accessed January 1, 2018).

19. See, for example, *Karsten Nowrot, Normative Ordnungen und
private Wirkungsmacht* (Berlin: BWV Verlag, 2006), p. 636 f.,
not as a replacement for state legislative procedures but as
complementary to them.

CHAPTER 2

A FINE STATE OF AFFAIRS

BAZON BROCK

Thinking about the common good requires the identification of those associations whose "good" is to be promoted: forms of association such as anthropologists attribute to tribes, or communities as described by St Paul, or the middle classes in European urban development, or the models of the state and states as conceived by Hegel as absolute spirit or "mortal god." (The fact that the gods of the Egyptians, Assyrians, Persians, Hittites, Greeks, and Romans died is more significant than how they came into the world.)

For believers, not just in the Pauline community, the common good focuses on the claim of validity of their own religion, and each individual is encouraged to implement and strengthen this claim by sacrificing their own life, since life is not the ultimate prize, but rather the afterlife. For burghers who lived under the protection of the lord of the manor (*Burgherr* in German), the common good is the preservation of this protective space and protection from the arbitrary ambushes of private feudalism (or capitalism today), as the common good can be seen as the implementation of a law to which all citizens subject themselves in all aspects of their lives. This creates freedom for all in the acknowledgment and implementation of the law that applies to all and operates for the benefit of all. This can be seen in the expression *Stadtluft macht frei*[*]— today this understanding of freedom is still conveyed in the general recognition of traffic regulations, as observing these rules enables the free use of the roads in the first place. For members of tribes and believers, the common good is thus something you are prepared to sacrifice your life for.

For citizens, the common good means freedom for all citizens.

---

[*] *Stadtluft macht frei* [city air makes you free] refers to a German medieval legal principle, whereby serfs were deemed free of their former masters' ownership if they succeeded in living for one year and a day in the city. [translator's note]

For the student nation (medieval *Landsmannschaften* or fraternities), which was organized like a state, and which includes all the communities in its territory, the common good can be seen as an unconditional mission against the destructive power of time, against the fury of oblivion. It was and is a question of ensuring perpetuity—at least a millennium—through greatness, power, and glory.

The common good of all nations together is the preservation of humanity against the blind actionism of evolution. The latter's failed endeavors increase our amazement at what has been achieved to date, that is our amazement at the power of spirit, thus metaphysics in the face of the arbitrary rule of natural laws.

Thus the common good is described:

1. In the sense of evolutionary fitness, as an advantage created by the readiness to die in order to be remembered, and that means becoming an example of the recognition of the claim that your community is everything, through your readiness to give up your life for it;

2. As the guarantee of citizens' freedom under the rule of legal equality that applies to all and operates for the benefit of all;

3. As a service to the transgenerational guarantee of permanence, in order to escape the meaningless logic of creation as destruction (supposed "creative destruction") by enacting perpetuity (in institutions such as museums, archives, the hermeneutics of conservatism, the emotional attachment to monuments, and the guarantee of permanence as exemplified by graveyards and Germany's Basic Law, Article 79, section 3 [the eternity clause], or the takeover of ongoing costs in industry, known in German as "eternal costs" [*Ewigkeitskosten*]).

To summarize: today, the common good is that which gives members of a community the freedom to develop their individuality, or constitutionally enables the community to live with a multiplicity of religious convictions without the competition that results in obliteration. This means that the common good applies to the development, education, and encouragement of individuality. This is neither dialectical play nor an insistence on paradoxes, since identity (that is, what is common to the members of a community) can be achieved only through the acknowledgement of those from whom one wants to differentiate oneself. In fact, the formation of identity as a goal of education and encouragement means, in complete opposition to the traditional definition of extraordinariness or superiority, the permanent obligation to and acknowledgement of other people, as only by doing so is the particular singularity of those constituting the difference possible.

Successful communities are either associations of those prepared to die, or of highly developed individuals who feel obligations to shared responsibilities by virtue of their autonomy. Natural involuntary communities are unstable because they lack the ability to adapt to changed circumstances. Every individual's early socialization takes place in such involuntary communities, which we call cultures. However, from a certain level of the individual's development onwards, the collective's identity is no longer in a position to support him or her as an individual: once the individual can recognize the logic of the decline of rigid communities, his or her superior knowledge obtained through individuality forces the community to make changes in the name of guaranteeing the common good, that is the survival of the community. Advanced individuals must thus put aside their traditional cultures if, for example as scientists and artists, they want to acquire the knowledge that qualifies them to look at their own community or culture from a detached, outside point of view. Since 1400, it has been the Europeans' unique characteristic to be expected to and to be able to practice natural philosophy (today's natural sciences) and the *septem artes liberales* (today's arts) no longer as members of a tribe or a particular culture, since one practiced and still practices chemistry (whether as a pharmacist, an alchemist, or a chemical engineer) not as a Jew, a Chinese person, or a Christian, but simply as a chemist, that is within the new communities of universal civilization and no longer within local cultures. This way of pursuing the common good of humanity—a random and thus highly fragile product of evolution—focuses on truth as a basis for tackling life's challenges (pain relief, reducing the burden of work, preventing the natural, sometimes fatal struggle for scarce resources).

The constitutional principle that everything, even property, can only be justified by a commitment to the common good, implies therefore that the individual's pursuit of happiness can only succeed under the supremacy of the common good—what Jeremy Bentham called the greatest good for the greatest number. Thus, general egotism does not create the altruistic collective unconditionally, as the first generation of classical political economists assumed. Regulations must be implemented, under which egotism can flourish without risking the destruction of weaker egotists by more radical ones, as this would mean the end of the pursuit of happiness for all, and would thus be a counterproductive destruction. Since time immemorial, meaning both logically and naturally, democracy has been considered a guarantor of upholding the pursuit of happiness, that is the pursuit of meaningful life in the daily fulfillment of the duty of asserting a law that applies to all and operates for the benefit of all. This means the duty to be just. Accordingly, in democracies and constitutional states the common good is the all-encompassing commitment to justice.

How far this notion of all right-thinking people has vanished today can be demonstrated in the most banal of everyday incidents. In almost every restaurant, even the most expensive, guests are subjected to inconsiderate, musical noise. When asking for this nuisance to be switched off or at least turned down, one receives the response that other guests like this musical embellishment. When the other guests deny this, the staff refer to the boss's orders that every guest has to put up with it, even though the latter thinks he's guaranteeing the existence of the restaurant in the first place by paying money for the food. In shopping malls, music pounds simultaneously out of every store, each with their own program that music psychologists say removes customers' will to resist, thus rendering them easily gullible when it comes to making purchases. The director of a chemical factory justifies the consumption of unsafe riverbank filtrate taken from a nearby industrial site as drinking water by referring to his own family, who would also have to consume this water if they lived nearby. In short, the Kafkaesque vision of justice as an arbitrary power that affects everyone seems to have prevailed even in the case of high-level legal judgments. It is a fine confirmation of humanity's hope that the common good will triumph as justice.

CHAPTER 3

WHO DEFINES THE COMMON GOOD?

WOLFGANG SCHÖN

We live in politically uncertain times. Under the slogan "America First," the US seems to have abandoned its natural, fundamental solidarity with its Western allies. In the West, the European Union is faced with Brexit—and with it the open question of its future relationship with the UK—and at the same time it must resist the disintegration of new constitutional systems in the East. NATO is experiencing serious conflicts between its members, in particular in the relationship between the European allies and their important partner, Turkey. Natural solidarity between nations seems to be a thing of the past.

Nevertheless, in most societies—but also at a European and a global level—there is positive encouragement towards joint commitment, to promote the common good and also to put aside individual interests in order to do this. In Germany, despite the perversion of "the community before the individual" during the National Socialist period, it is still widely recognized today that such public-spiritedness is part of the "glue" required of every social organization. If this principle is losing its efficacy, however, we must focus on two developments.

First, the common good is inconceivable without reference to a real community. This may be defined as a family or a community, as a nation-state or as a supranational union, perhaps even as a global society. Every individual is a member of overlapping communities and is thus subject to parallel or competing demands when it comes to the common good. Indeed, the debate sparked in 2017 by the French President Macron's suggestions for a deepening of the European Union, as well as the search for solutions to international migration or the wrangling over the Paris climate accord, confront the citizen with the question of whether they should be thinking and acting first and foremost as a citizen of a specific nation, as a European citizen or even as a citizen of the world? Is the lesson to be drawn from Brexit more or less Europe? Or a *"Europe à deux vitesses"*?

While political discourse tends to blur any possible conflicts between these perspectives on the common good ("what benefits Europe, benefits Germany too"), within the population, by contrast, it fuels uncertainty. It is also striking that political objectives formulated by German policies genuinely in the European interest are often perceived by other Member States as the expression of German interests (or at least as Germany's aspiration to control the definition of European interests). Is it reasonable—as Martin Schulz said at the SPD conference in early December 2017—to want to set up a "United States of Europe" in just a few years' time? Would it be "more honest" to simply emphasize the national point of view? This is the aim of the US President's senior advisors, Gary D. Cohn and H.R. McMaster, when they wrote in the *Wall Street Journal* in terms of US policies, "that the world is not a 'global community' but an arena where nations, nongovernmental actors, and businesses engage and compete for advantage."

As unconvincing as it may be to want to realize the "global common good" on all political fronts, a general re-nationalization of interests is equally incapable of solving the world's real problems. It seems right to focus on different political reference systems depending on the topic: climate change and migration touch on global public goods, while social security or education systems are typically formulated within a national framework. Defense and security policy, like trade and economic policy, demand regional and supranational structures. The citizen will have to be prepared to think and act as a German/Frenchman/Englishman, a European, or a global citizen depending on the topic—otherwise their thinking will be too small or too big. So it is the right thing, despite the resistance of the US President, to adhere to the Paris climate accord. And it also remains the right thing to work on finding European solutions to the international refugee crisis. Finally, amid all the furore of the Brexit negotiations, we should never forget how extremely important the civilizing effect of solidarity (as well as solidarity in security policy and economics) between the countries on the continent of Europe and the UK will remain, regardless of changes in the underlying institutional framework.

Second, the common good has no exact definition; it must constantly be concretized in political discourse. But the providers and mechanisms of this discourse—the political parties and representative democracy—are distrusted more and more. The traditional systems of party politics are crumbling—from France to Austria and far beyond. Elections are won against "the system." Even in Germany, the voters in the 2017 general election entrusted no single party and also no natural coalition of particular parties with the power to govern.

However, if political or intellectual elites occasionally tell voters that they have made the "wrong" decision, the elites must be asked what criteria they are applying to results that have been produced through democratically correct processes. Are citizens wrong—or does the constitutional system create the wrong incentives with regard to the political process? And yet making politics "scientific" and assigning unrealistic tasks to an expertocracy would not provide an alternative. The accusation of dominance by an elite—and this should not be overlooked—is often made less against the truly rich and powerful than against experts in public service, in political parties and advisory committees, and, last but not least, in universities.

However, as individuals in an increasing number of countries are claiming to represent the common good "over and above" all political parties, this must give cause for concern—beyond any sympathy or antipathy towards those individuals—to those who would like to see politics as a succession of rational decisions. It has always been a winning formula for dictators at the start of their careers to pretend to be the only legitimate providers and executors of the will of the people.

It is perhaps high time to explore the possibilities of direct democracy more intensively in many countries, including Germany. It is not just every four or five years that the citizen must take responsibility for the common good. However, this means taking a shrewd look at the experiences of other countries: what is the difference between the successful reconnection of politics with the people through referendums in Switzerland and the Brexit referendum, which was fuelled by hysteria? Which topics lend themselves to informed grassroots treatment—and which do not? A revival of the citizen's public-spiritedness will not take place if they are not polled specifically about the common good.

CHAPTER 4

THE COMMON GOOD IN TAX LAW

RUDOLF MELLINGHOFF

Like justice, the common good is one of those concepts that is widely recognized yet extremely difficult to comprehend. Entire libraries have been written on the substance and specification of the common good. The idea of the common good has been debated throughout all eras of European history and in all present-day states.[1] It is a highly abstract concept that eludes a conclusive definition, but is nevertheless regarded as a goal of any state activity. The concept of the common good is not only used repeatedly in political rhetoric but it is also invoked in the constitutional state as a way of justifying the actions of government.

Germany's Federal Constitutional Court (FCC) also uses the concept of the common good very frequently: the common good is referred to in over 570 decisions published in the FCC's court reports.**

The common good plays an important role particularly in the area of financial and tax law. In this context our first question is whether the case law of the FCC can provide a substantive specification of the common good. We can then show in which areas of financial and tax law the common good acquires particular importance.

I. SUBSTANTIVE SPECIFICATION OF THE COMMON GOOD

The common good has an established role in financial and tax law. The FCC mentions the concept of the common good in over 300 decisions in the area of tax law. For example, the constitutional provisions of the Basic Law governing public finances, based on clearly defined forms and committed to these forms, substantiates an element of justice with regard to the common good.[2] In several decisions, the FCC defends tax law's

---

** The figures quoted refer to all decisions published by the FCC.

deviations from the principle of equality in taxation, citing the interests of the common good. Even legitimate expectations, based on the rule of law, are subject to the common good. Yet, it is acknowledged that granting full protection to the continuation of the present legal situation would in important areas paralyze a legislature that is dedicated to the common good, and would resolve the conflict between the reliability of the legal system and the necessity of its amendment with regard to a change in living conditions unjustifiably at the expense of the legal system's adaptability.[3] Even in closed cases a retrospective intervention is permissible if the overriding interests of the common good, following the principle of legal certainty, require a retrospective alteration.[4]

1. SPECIFICATION OF THE COMMON GOOD IN THE CONSTITUTION

Initially, it is unclear what is to be understood specifically by the interests of the common good. The common good is often explained in terms of the realization of constitutional goals. The common good is mentioned explicitly in Article 14(2), sentence 2 of the Basic Law (GG), which states that the use of property "shall also serve the public good." However, the FCC not only refers to the common good in its case law in relation to Article 14 GG, but in general considers that the protection of fundamental rights is an important goal of the common good.

The protection of life and health (Article 2[2] GG) and of the natural foundations of life (Article 20a GG) are particularly important constitutional values; accordingly, laws that serve to protect these fundamental rights pursue high-value interests of the common good.[5] This has been emphasized most recently by the FCC in its decision with regard to the nuclear energy opt-out. However, this is long-settled case law of the Court.[6] Measures in tax law that favor environmental protection are also explicitly justified as serving the common good.[7] In general, health protection measures, as well as preventive measures or addiction prevention, are supported by common good objectives.[8]

However, it is not only the fundamental right to life and health that is derived from fundamental rights as an important interest of the common good. In general, the fundamental duties and functions of the state specify the common good. For example, the duty to promote science and research (Article 5[3] GG) is an interest of the common good directly derived from the Basic Law.[9] The special protection afforded to marriage and the family by the Basic Law in Article 6(1) also specifies the common good as defined in the Basic Law.[10]

In addition to fundamental rights, the state's own objectives serve the common good. The institutional guarantee of equal opportunity decision-making is a necessary condition of democracy and thus an important interest of the common good which also plays a role in tax law.[11] A connection with democratic decision-making is made if the favoring of individual groups' special interests is seen as inimical to the common good.[12] Limiting unfettered competition is generally considered an interest of the common good. The legislature may restrict the freedom of competitive behavior in order to keep competition within limits that are compatible with the common good.[13]

The principle of the welfare state in particular grants the legislature important measures for advancing the common good. It is therefore accepted that taxes may be aligned with taxpayers' needs.[14] Income tax law above all is based on the principles of social justice. The subjective net principle, tax exemption of subsistence level incomes, family taxation, taking account of special expenses and exceptional costs and, historically, progressive taxation are expressions of the principle of the welfare state and tax law's commitment to the common good.[15]

Reference is made to the rule of law when the functioning of tax law jurisdiction as part of the overall administration of justice represents an extremely important interest of the common good.[16] In this context we should also mention fairness in taxation, the fight against tax avoidance, as well as prevention of the abuse of social benefits.[17] Efficiency in the criminal justice system is part of the rule of law and, at the same time, part of the essential conditions for the state to function.[18] The system of legal process, legal certainty, and greater clarity are interests of the common good[19] that can be derived from the rule of law.

2. SUPPLEMENTARY GENERAL SPECIFICATIONS OF THE COMMON GOOD

However, Germany's Basic Law itself contains only a partial specification of the common good. Alongside human dignity, duties to protect as laid down by fundamental rights, and state aims, the Basic Law contains important indications of what the Federal Republic of Germany considers to be the common good. But this does not exhaust the meaning contained within the common good. Rather, there are numerous other measures that serve the general public and are cited in the case law of the FCC as interests of the common good. We will mention here just a few examples taken from the FCC's case law in the field of tax legislation.

The prohibition of specific commercial activities by legal professionals is regarded as an interest of the common good because of the importance of the administration of justice.[20] The ban on the use of additions to the professional title of "tax consultant" is justified with reference to important interests of the common good, because it protects against the dilution of official designations and titles and, to avoid misleading those seeking legal tax advice in particular, clarifies which designations and accolades have been professionally awarded. The latter can thus claim an official guarantee of their fundamental standards of quality and inspire especial confidence.[21]

In addition to the simplification of tax law, another paramount interest of the common good is the aim of managing the financial burden of Germany's reunification. The reparation of National Socialist injustice also represents a particularly important objective of the common good.[22] However, the simple intention of generating state revenue is not, in itself, an interest of the common good that can routinely overcome the protection of taxpayers' legitimate interests, because this goal might be achieved by any means, even including erratic and arbitrary taxation. Conversely, the state interest in compensating for unexpected revenue shortfalls by amending tax laws or by correcting certain impacts of tax law is an important interest of the common good.[23]

Economic policy objectives also fall under the aegis of the common good.[24] For example, the interests of the construction industry, and especially of the housing industry, serve the common good. An overriding interest of the common good in particular is the provision of a sufficient amount of housing, which addresses a basic existential requirement.[25]

The FCC recognizes that the common good not only determines the actions of the state in the more narrow sense, but that it is also fundamentally important for the actions of society.[26] The FCC specifically mentions the context of and obligation towards the common good in connection with the inheritance tax burden on medium-sized enterprises.

This cursory overview of the FCC's case law on the concept of the common good—in particular in financial and tax law—produces no clear outline for defining what is meant by the common good. On the one hand, the Basic Law, in particular the duties of protection and state objectives based on fundamental rights, provides important indications as to what is meant by an interest of the common good. Beyond this, however, there are also numerous other interests that the FCC considers as serving the common good. Depending on the context in which the concept is used, almost any state measure can be justified with reference to the common good. This is based on the belief that the common good is the necessary goal of every state activity.[27]

It is appropriate, therefore, alongside the values of the constitution, to consider both competence when it comes to defining the common good and its legitimation through procedure.[28] Since there is no universally valid definition of the common good, it is important to examine who has the competence to specify the substance of the common good, and by what procedure this takes place. In a democracy, it is the elected parliament that defines the interest of the common good in more detail and translates it into laws. Democratic decision-making and parliamentary procedure provide legitimation based on the will of the people. The competence and procedure of parliamentary democracy supports the substantive quality of the decision and encourages its acceptability.

The essential corrective in this context, however, is a constitutional court, which ensures that decisions taken by the state conform to the Basic Law. In so doing, the parliamentary legislature acquires further leeway in determining the interest of the common good, which, however, is limited by the provisions of the Basic Law. It is up to the parliamentary legislature to consider first of all the obligations and state objectives based on fundamental rights. Beyond that, however, the legislature is not prevented from defining additional interests of the common good.

II. ADVANCEMENT OF THE COMMON GOOD IN TAX LAW

Specified in this way, the common good is advanced in tax law in different ways. In general, tax law complies with issues concerning the welfare state and the rule of law. It has already been pointed out that, especially in income tax law, the welfare state has an influence on the structure of the law. This applies above all to the subsistence level of the taxpayer and their family, progressive taxation, and the consideration of living costs such as special expenses and exceptional costs. But in sales tax law, too, the interest of the common good means that individual sales are either tax-exempt or subject to a reduced rate of tax. The reduced tax rate is also justified by interests of the common good that are influenced by the welfare state. In principle, goods and services that cover the essential needs of the end user should be taxed at a reduced rate. To the extent that tax breaks cannot be regarded as an exemption for essential needs, they are subsidies or tax breaks designed to reduce international competitive disadvantages, which, like the social and control standards in income tax law, are justified by the interests of the common good.

In tax law, the common good is specified in particular by two techniques implemented by parliamentary legislature. On the one hand, there are deviations from standard taxation, which are intended to advance the interest of the common good. On the other hand, in tax law, the common good has been regulated in a positive legal way in the taxation relating to non-profit organizations.

1. JUSTIFYING SUBSIDIES AND CONTROLS FOR REASONS OF THE COMMON GOOD

Tax law is largely defined by the general principle of equality and thus by the principle of equal burdening. Former President of Germany Roman Herzog called the principle of equality before the law the "Magna Carta" of tax law. An appropriate distribution of the tax burden and uniformity of taxation are central concerns of every tax system. Thomas Hobbes said that people felt less oppressed by the tax burden as such than by its unequal distribution. The acceptability of taxation stands and falls by its equality of burdening. The general equality of burdening is often more important to taxpayers than the amount of the tax burden in each individual case. The principle of equality before the law in its sectoral application to current tax law implies that each resident is called upon equally to finance general functions of the state, according to their financial resources.

One justification for deviating from the principle of equality of burdening is when the legislature wants to advance the interests of the common good using tax subsidies and controls. The FCC basically leaves it up to the legislature to decide which interests of the common good it considers eligible. It also gives the legislature generous room for maneuver when it comes to determining the extent of tax advantages. If there are sufficient reasons related to the common good, relief can, in exceptional cases, in a constitutionally permissible manner, even lead to the complete exclusion of certain tax items from taxation.[29]

However, the appeal to interests of the common good does not justify every violation of the principle of equality. Rather, during implementation, the FCC demands compliance with the principle of consistency and thus a certain basic rationality of the law. The legislature may not distribute its services according to non-objective criteria, that is not arbitrarily. The purpose must be sufficiently clear in law. In addition, the circle of beneficiaries of a measure must be appropriately delimited and balanced.[30] Unequal tax burdens cannot be justified using the financial needs of the state alone or a tight budgetary situation.[31] For these reasons, the FCC has repeatedly regarded tax privileges as well as controls as unconstitutional because they did not meet these requirements.

2. THE LAW GOVERNING PUBLIC-BENEFIT ORGANIZATIONS AND DONATIONS AS A WAY OF ADVANCING THE COMMON GOOD

The common good is specified in particular in the tax law governing public-benefit organizations and donations. For entities that pursue public-benefit, charitable, or religious aims, there are privileges provided by individual tax laws. Today public-benefit law is playing an increasingly important role. There are over 600,000 public-benefit organizations in Germany alone, and their number continues to increase. Almost half of all Germans are members of public-benefit associations, and in the case of a third of these associations the number of members has increased by comparison with 2012. Sport is the largest group of organizations at 22 percent. However, the greatest increase in membership has been recorded among associations that represent citizens' or consumers' interests. Traditional associations are increasingly supplemented by new kinds of organization. Since the start of the 1990s, it can be said that there has been a veritable boom in newly established organizations, for example foundations. Half of all foundations in Germany were set up between the beginning of 2000 and the end of 2010. A further growth area in public-benefit organizations is associations of "Friends": one association in five (22 percent) is a "Friends" group. They exist in all areas of activity, but at over 40 percent they can be found most frequently in the area of education. They support kindergartens, schools, universities, and individual university departments, as well as music schools and community colleges.[32]

Tax relief or tax exemption based on the common good is almost as old as tax itself. In the era of the Franconian Empire (c. 5th–9th centuries), certain actions that served the community (particularly, at that time, protecting the territory by serving as a mounted soldier, fortifying the city, and compulsory labor) led to exemption from "Bede and Stiura" (taxes paid to the lord of the manor), because these services were accepted as sufficient and full services rendered to emperor and king.[33] In the 17th century, when the idea emerged of universal, equitable taxation, tax exemption for comparable alternative services rendered to the state became simultaneously acceptable. From this, the idea of "public-benefit equalization" developed in the 19th century: it is still in use today, and is applied to charitable, religious, and other public-benefit purposes.[34]

These tax breaks in public-benefit law are intended to stimulate the private, altruistic advancement of the common good and thus relieve the burden on the tax authorities. The idea is that this is not a tax subsidy, but an alternative to paying tax. The state grants a tax break on elements of the taxpayer's income, which the latter uses not for private benefit but for the benefit of all.[35] For this reason, the tax relief provisions governed by the tax law governing public-benefit organizations are also justified on the basis of tax substitution.[36] At the same time, public-benefit law is an expression of the principle of subsidiarity, in which the state respects private initiative and social self-regulation. Public-benefit activities can partially or even wholly replace state activities, thus dispensing with the tax-based funding of functions that serve the common good.[37] In so doing, the tax system respects the activities of its citizens based on civil rights, as carried out by them in the interests of the common good. However, the advancement of the common good alone is not sufficient to justify tax relief, because the individual's economic activity basically serves the general public as well. For this reason, a fundamental condition of public-benefit law is altruistic service to the general public. Only if activities serving the common good are rendered without expectation of return or a particular advantage are there grounds for tax exemption.[38] The condition that it must be of benefit to the general public precludes an exclusive circle of special interests from benefiting.[39] Endeavors that violate the principle of equality before the law,[40] or that are directed against the free, democratic constitution of the Federal Republic of Germany,[41] or against constitutionally guaranteed freedoms[41] can also not be accepted as benefiting the general public.[42]

Under current law, tax privileges are granted if an entity directly and exclusively pursues public-benefit, charitable, or religious purposes (Section 51[1] Fiscal Code of Germany). Today, the individual public-benefit purposes are enumerated in Section 52(2) Fiscal Code of Germany. These include the advancement of science and research; of religion; of public health; assistance to young and old people; of art and culture; of upbringing, adult education and vocational training; of nature conservation and landscape management; of public welfare; relief for people persecuted on political, racial, or religious grounds; the advancement of internationalism; of the protection of animals; of development cooperation; of equal rights for men and women; of the protection of marriage and the family; of crime prevention; of sport; of local heritage and traditions; of animal husbandry; and the general advancement of democratic government and of active citizenship.

Thus, if a variety of activities and leisure pursuits or fellowship, sociability, and fun can benefit fiscally, today's advancement of public benefit has to some extent moved some distance away from the original idea.[43] If we classify today's public-benefit law into various ideal types of tax-privileged activity,[44] not all of them meet the basic ideas of public benefit.[45] The idea of substituting government tasks is satisfied by competing common good tasks that perform such public functions, whose form and content are also the responsibility of the state (for example, the advancement of education, development cooperation, or the advancement of science and research). Pluralistic common good tasks, which include the charitable, pedagogical, or cultural services of private individuals, also supplement the functions of government and therefore fulfill the traditional notion of public benefit (for example the advancement of art and culture, the protection and preservation of historical monuments, the advancement of international understanding).

There can be ambivalence when it comes to deciding upon types of political activity. On the one hand, organizations that pursue special political interests can claim that their specific goals are accepted as of public benefit under Section 52(2) Fiscal Code of Germany (for example, the advancement of nature conservation, of development cooperation, the advancement of active citizenship). On the other hand, general political activity, influencing political opinion, and the advancement of political parties do not in principle serve public-benefit purposes. Funding political parties' formation of general political opinion is justified under Article 21(1) of the Basic Law, which states that political parties shall participate in the formation of the political will of the people. Party funding is subject to certain constitutional restrictions and is thus regulated separately. However, general political activity by a tax-privileged entity is still permissible if the engagement with political processes takes place within the framework of requiring and permitting the advocacy of statutory aims and their implementation, and if the views held by the entity about its statutory aims are objective and factually based, and the entity acts in a party-politically neutral way.[46] The question of whether and to what extent a politically focused entity, such as Attac, which is critical of globalization, can generally be accepted as serving the public benefit, has not yet been fully resolved.[47] The public-benefit law is often viewed critically when it favors organizations that advance activities associated with self-fulfillment and leisure. In the case of organizations promoting sport, in particular, the question arises as to whether these are not activities that are more of personal than of public benefit. This is also true in light of the fact that physical exercise usually serves self-fulfillment, and that even chess and tournament bridge[48] are considered eligible for support. With the recognition of leisure activities, the law as it currently stands is moving away from the original idea of public-benefit law.

III. OUTLOOK

This brief overview shows that the common good is firmly established in financial and tax law. Admittedly, an analysis of the case law of the FCC has shown that the concept of the common good is difficult to comprehend. On the other hand, the legislature expressly takes into account the interests of the common good in tax law in a variety of ways. In the case of deviations from uniformity of taxation based on ability to pay, the common good serves in particular as a justification of social and control standards. However, public-benefit law, which provides far-reaching tax privileges or tax exemptions for the pursuit of public-benefit, charitable, or religious purposes, is of particular significance.

In recent times, public-benefit law has been gaining in importance. This is shown by the steadily growing number of public-benefit associations, foundations, or other kinds of organization. Activities in the area of public-benefit law show that many citizens are willing to get involved in community life. Many questions still remain to be answered in the future. On the one hand there is the question of whether and to what extent the general political activity of NGOs should be given tax benefits. Moreover, increasing globalization poses further challenges when it comes to taking account of the common good in tax law. If we justify the current tax relief situation by saying that certain activities supplement or replace state activities, this means that public-benefit law is restricted to the state in question. On the other hand, European law calls for Europe-wide recognition of public-benefit activities.[49] Thus the debate about the interests of the common good in tax law will remain an exciting topic even in the future.

Notes

1. Josef Isensee in *Handbuch des Staatsrechts*, vol. IV, ed. by J. Isensee and P. Kirchhof, 3rd edn. (Heidelberg: C.F. Müller, 2006), para. 71, note 1.

2. Federal Constitutional Court, Order of April 13, 2017 – 2

BvL 6/13 – *Neue Juristische Wochenschrift* (*NJW*), p. 2249, note 58.

3. Federal Constitutional Court, Order of October 10, 2012 – 1 BvL 6/07 –, BVerfGE 132, 302, note 45.

4. Federal Constitutional Court, Order of December 17, 2013 – 1 BvL 5/08 –, BVerfGE 135, 1, note 65.

5. Federal Constitutional Court, Order of December 6, 2016 – 1 BvR 2821/11 –, BVerfGE 143, 246, note 303.

6. Federal Constitutional Court, Order of February 16, 2000 – 1 BvR 242/91 –, BVerfGE 102, 1, note 50.

7. Federal Constitutional Court, Non-acceptance Order of July 25, 2007 – 1 BvR 1031/07 –, *Deutsches Verwaltungsblatt* (2007), p. 1097.

8. Federal Constitutional Court, Non-acceptance Order of September 3, 2009 – 1 BvR 2384/08 –, *Höchstrichterliche Finanzsprechung* (2010), p. 177, note 40.

9. Federal Constitutional Court, Order of April 24, 1996 – 1 BvR 712/86 –, BVerfGE 94, 268, note 131.

10. Federal Constitutional Court, Order of May 29, 1990 – 1 BvL 20/84 –, BVerfGE 82, 60, note 89.

11. Federal Constitutional Court, Order of April 17, 2008 – 2 BvL 4/05 –, BVerfGE 121, 108.

12. Federal Constitutional Court, Order of January 28, 2014 – 2 BvR 1561/12 –, BVerfGE 135, 155, note 171.

13. Federal Constitutional Court Order of January 27, 2010 – 2 BvR 2185/04 –, BVerfGE 125, 141, note 88.

14. Federal Constitutional Court, Order of December 8, 2009 – 2 BvR 758/07 –, BVerfGE 125, 104, note 80.

15. Rudolf Mellinghoff in *Mitverantwortung von Bürger und Staat für ein gerechtes Steuerrecht*, ed. by Jürgen Brandt (Stuttgart, Munich: Richard Boorberg Verlag, 2006), p. 31 ff.

16. Federal Constitutional Court's Chamber Decision (accepted) of August 23, 2013 – 1 BvR 2912/11 –, *NJW* (2013), p. 3357, note 30.

17. Federal Constitutional Court, Rejection of Interim Measures of March 22, 2005 – 1 BvQ 2/05 –, BVerfGE 112, 284, note 49.

18. On this, see Herbert Landau, "Die Pflicht des Staates zum Erhalt einer funktionstüchtigen Strafrechtspflege" in *Neue Zeitschrift für Strafrecht (NStZ)* (2007), p. 121.

19. Federal Constitutional Court, Non-acceptance Order of August 23, 2010 – 1 BvR 1632/10 –, *NJW* (2010), p. 3291, note 12.

20. Federal Constitutional Court, Non-acceptance Order of December 6, 2011 – 1 BvR 2280/11 –, *NJW* (2012), p. 993, note 20.

21. Federal Constitutional Court, Non-acceptance Order of June 9, 2010 – 1 BvR 1198/10 –, *NJW* (2010), p. 3705, note 12.

22. Federal Constitutional Court, Judgment of November 23, 1999 – 1 BvF 1/94 –, BVerfGE 101, 239, note 105.

23. Federal Constitutional Court, Order of February 5, 2002 – 2 BvR 305/93 –, BVerfGE 105, 17, note 82.

24. Federal Constitutional Court, Order of May 6, 2014 – 2 BvR 1139/12 –, BVerfGE 136, 194, note 139.

25. Federal Constitutional Court, Order of November 7, 2006 – 1 BvL 10/02 –, BVerfGE 117, 1, note 158.

26. Isensee, op. cit., note 73.

27. Decision of July 17, 2003 – 2 BvL 1/99 –, BVerfGE 108, 186, note 147.

28. Cf. Isensee, op. cit., note 89 ff.

29. Federal Constitutional Court, Order of November 7, 2006 – 1 BvL 10/02 –, BVerfGE 117, 1, note 98.

30. Federal Constitutional Court, Judgment of December 17, 2014 – 1 BvL 21/12 –, BVerfGE 138, 136, note 125 ff. with further references.

31. Federal Constitutional Court, Order of January 15, 2014 – 1 BvR 1656/09 –, BVerfGE 135, 126, note 79.

32. All these statistics have been taken from ZiviZ-Surveys 2017: http://www.ziviz.info/projekte/ziviz-survey (accessed January 2, 2018).

33. Stephan Geserich in *Leitgedanken des Rechts*, vol. II, ed. by H. Kube, R. Mellinghoff, and G. Morgenthaler et al. (Heidelberg et al.: C.F. Müller, 2013), para 162 "Gemeinnützigkeit," note 2.

34. Ibid., note 5.

35. Paul Kirchhof "Gemeinnützigkeit" ed. by Monika Jachmann in *Deutsche Steuerjuristische Gesellschaft (DStJG)*, vol. 26 (2003), p. 1 (5).

36. Roman Seer in Jachmann (ed.), op. cit., p. 11 (33).

37. Ibid., p. 22.

38. Geserich, op. cit., note 9.

39. Federal Fiscal Court, Judgment of July 23, 2003 – I R 41/03 –, BFHE 203, 305, *Bundessteuerblatt (BStBl)*, vol. II (2005), p. 443; on the limit in amounts of member contributions and admission fees compare 1.1 AEAO [General Tax Code Application Decree] with Fiscal Code of Germany, para. 52.

40. Federal Fiscal Court, Judgment of May 17, 2017 – V R 52/15 –, *Deutsches Steuerrecht* (2017), p. 1749 (Masonic lodge).

41. Federal Fiscal Court, Judgment of April 11, 2012 – I R 11/11 –, BFHE 237, 22, *BStBl*, vol. II (2013), p. 146 (Islamic–Salafist Union).

42. Federal Fiscal Court, Judgment of October 16, 1991 – I B 16/91 –, BFH/NV 1992, 505.

43. One example among many is Josef Isensee, "Gemeinwohl und Bürgersinn im Steuerstaat des Grundgesetzes: Gemeinnützigkeit als Bewährungsprobe des Steuerrechts vor der Verfassung" in *Das akzeptierte Grundgesetz : Festschrift für Günter Dürig zum 70. Geburtstag*, ed. by Hartmut Maurer et al. (Munich: C.H. Beck, 1990), p. 33 ff.

44. Essential on this typology is Josef Isensee and Brigitte Knobbe-Keuk, "Reform des Gemeinnützigkeits- und Spendenrechts" in *Gutachten der Unabhängigen Sachverständigenkommission zur Prüfung des Gemeinnützigkeits- und Spendenrechts*, ed. by Darstellung und Analyse des geltenden Gemeinnützigkeitsrechts: Bundesministerium der Finanzen (Bonn: Stollfuß, 1988), p. 331 ff.

45. Cf. the following: Isensee, op. cit., p. 47 ff.

46. Federal Fiscal Court, Judgment of March 20, 2017 – X R 13/15 –, BFHE 257, 486, *BStBl*, vol. II (2017), p. 1110.

47. Finance Court, Hesse, Judgment of November 10, 2016 – 4 K 179/16 –, *Deutsches Steuerrecht – Entscheidungsdienst* (2017), p. 1128; revision was approved by the Federal Fiscal Court.

48. Federal Fiscal Court, Judgment of February 9, 2017 – V R 70/14 –, BFHE 257, 12, *BStBl*, vol. II (2017), p. 1106.

49. Geserich, op. cit, note 12.

CHAPTER 5

GERMANY'S FEDERAL BUDGET 2030: HOW TO STAY ON THE ROAD TO ECONOMIC AND SOCIAL SUCCESS

JENS SPAHN

How can Germany's 2030 federal budget stay on the road to economic and social success? This assumes that Germany as a whole will remain economically and socially successful, and includes the acknowledgment that at present we live in a Germany that is more economically successful than it has been for a long time—with so much prosperity, so many opportunities, so much freedom, and so much mobility. This does not mean that there are not some people who have to count every euro every day in order to make ends meet. But nevertheless we should acknowledge that never before in Germany has there been so much economic power and so much prosperity, and that in total more people than ever before have been able to share in this success.

Germany's current budgetary situation is both globally and historically unique. In 1969, Franz Josef Strauss was the last Finance Minister to incur no new debt, and even that lasted just one year. For the next 45 years Germany ran up debt every year. The fact that now, for the fourth year in a row, the country has managed to get by with no new debt is something special. In the budget for the period up to 2021, which was agreed by the cabinet at the end of the last parliamentary term, we, the government (of which I am a part), anticipate the continuation of this policy. This would mean another eight years with no new debt.

This achievement not only has an inherent value, but it is above all a genuine provision for the future, contributing to intergenerational equity. Every businessperson knows that after the good years, bad years will arrive at some point. We should thus create a margin for the bad years during the good. Moreover, the new federal government inherits a budget with a surplus of 15 billion euros that has not yet been allocated. This is unique in the history of the Federal

Republic. We have already provided important economic and social incentives. When Wolfgang Schäuble became Finance Minister in 2009, we had a deficit of 80 billion euros per year—now we have surpluses. We have used the intervening period not only for budgetary consolidation, but also to provide incentives—in the areas of investment, infrastructure, as well as in the social sector. In the last few years, the Federal Republic of Germany has invested more than ever before.

We are even in the position—for example, in the case of the transport budget, which since the beginning of this parliamentary term has grown by over 40 percent—that we actually cannot spend any more money. And so we must talk about our planning procedure, as that too is a question of the future and the common good. Is the person who campaigns for nesting places for bats or frogs the only one doing something morally worthwhile? Or is the person who campaigns for jobs and infrastructure also doing something worthwhile? Ultimately this is a question of weighing up different public goods.

The federal government's total investment in education, science, and research has also been massively increased, but unfortunately this has been somewhat lost in the public perception. Over the last twelve years, federal research expenditure has risen from 7 to 17 billion euros, an increase of over 130 percent. This is how, in the budget, we are putting further significant emphasis on investing in our future sustainability.

The challenges of recent years have meant that we have had to invest more in our security. The Minister of the Interior's expenditure has increased by over 50 percent in the last four years—with a clear focus on the Federal Police, the Federal Criminal Police Office, and protection of the constitution. The question has also arisen of whether we now have enough police and judiciary to enforce law and order. The need for security, the desire to be able to get home safely in the dark at night, is a common social interest. And guaranteeing this security is the state's most essential task.

The same applies to external security. Spending in the Defense Department has increased by almost 20 percent, and there is a similar increase in the Foreign Aid Department. This extra expenditure is necessary because we all feel that the time of the peace dividend is over. What happens in Russia or the Middle East affects us too. And the impact on us and North Africa makes it necessary again to invest more in neighborhood policy, foreign aid, as well as external security, and, ideally, to coordinate this with our European partners. To cope with the influx of refugees and asylum seekers in 2017 alone we had to allocate 20 billion euros of federal spending. We can deal with this unexpected situation by planning to invest 20 billion euros a year—and without taking on any new debt. This too indicates the excellent and unique situation we are in right now. In addition, over the last few years we have implemented tax relief of around 12 billion euros.

Budgeting and budget implementation are always interesting and demanding processes of debate. There are some who talk about tax giveaways when taxes are lowered. But this is the wrong way to think about it. In the first place, when the citizen hands over their hard-earned money to the common good, this is an intrusion on their freedom. This creates a special responsibility when drawing up the federal budget. Every year the common good is defined anew as part of budget preparation in a deliberative process that takes place in parliament and the pre-political sphere.

For example, expenditure in the large "social" sphere has also increased in recent years. The principle of the welfare state is established in our Basic Law, and how this is to be actually expressed is renegotiated annually when spending is fixed for the coming year.

This process of negotiating the common good does not mean maximizing individual interests or simply adding them together. A fixed notion of the common good smacks of ideology or dictatorship. In our parliamentary democracy the term is constantly redefined in a deliberative, inquiring process.

This process is about ensuring a forum for debate that approximates as closely as possible to the ideas of Habermas and other thinkers who discuss ideal discourse and communication. Discussion must be fair and free, and no one should be given preferential treatment, although defining the common good may well disadvantage some individuals. A concrete example is an airport runway. While it is in the general interest—because of economic considerations, for example—that a runway be built, local residents are likely to be severely affected by disadvantages such as noise pollution. A defined common good will not be to everyone's satisfaction, but it is the result of a democratic and representative process, and therefore it is legitimate for a few to suffer disadvantages as a result.

The common good is an attempt to create the greatest added value with the least possible depreciation in value for individuals and other stakeholders. In this context, our demographic situation is an enormous challenge. In the general election of September 24, 2017, one in three voters was over 60 years old, and the average age of voters was 52. Of course, this also has an impact on the majority-voting system, and the question of which topics play a role in the election campaign. In addition, electoral participation among older people is very high by comparison with 18- to 35-year-olds. So a party manager, who wants to win as many votes as possible as easily as possible, focuses on topics that reach most potential voters, namely older people. This, in turn, has an impact on how the concept of the common good is developed and negotiated. In this process, the interests of younger people are naturally taken into account less, and they need other advocates. The latter are often to be found within the family, for example, when grandparents write to me, saying we need to "stand firm on pensions" in the interests of their grandchildren. But how we see things is not just a matter of age. And future prospects must be discussed again and again in majority processes, where the debt brake, for example, is enormously important. From 2020, federal states are no longer allowed to incur new debt. It is a restriction that politics has imposed upon itself, a restriction that is intended to limit economies' burdens on future generations. The sometimes harsh effects on individual budgets can already be felt today. In addition to the debt brake, we could consider changing electoral law in order to take greater account of the future in the process of democratic decision-making itself. For several years,

I have campaigned for a family voting right, in which parents represent their children's voting rights on their behalf. I know all the counter-arguments. There are many ways of dismantling the topic into specific issues straightaway. But the question of how better to take on board the interests of future generations in elections as basic democratic decisions in a represent-ative democracy, even institutionally, remains on the agenda. I am convinced that in light of ongoing demo-graphic change this will become even more urgent, because it will not always remain the case that one in three voters is over 60.

For the federal budget too, demographic change is one of the biggest challenges. This will be especially true from 2030, if Germany's current aging process continues. In 1964, there were almost 1.4 million births in Germany. All these people turned 50 three years ago. In 2014, approximately 700,000 children were born in Germany. This means we already know today that in about thirteen years 1.4 million people will retire, and yet not even half that number will enter the labor market. Of course, this is not without impact on the federal budget as the key component of state activity in Germany. We have to concentrate on major savings for the period between 2030 and 2060. And social systems are facing structural changes that we need to discuss over the next few years if we want to maintain our high standards and at the same time provide the younger generation with future prospects.

In light of these challenges, I am astonished to hear people saying that Germany no longer needs growth, and measuring happiness is enough. A Bundestag commission of inquiry has even looked into this. As a result, we are now compiling a happiness index and trying to keep up with Tibet, which is supposedly the happiest region in the world. But the truth is, we cannot pay pensions with happiness. Almost certainly we will continue to need economic growth in Germany, because we want to maintain prosperity, even in an aging society. That is why we are also looking at how to create the conditions for future growth, what incentives we need in digitalization, technological innovation, and infrastructure, and whether we are ready to think again when it comes to data protection or forms of work in the future. If life expectancy increases by six hours every day, we will have to work half an hour longer in the future to pay the balance. We must be able to discuss these issues, discarding the usual rapid reflexes we applied ten years ago. Stoking fears of poverty in old age may bring a deal of plaudits in the short term, but it does not solve any problems. The best example of this is the pension age of 63, which benefits mainly skilled, physically and mentally fit specialized male workers, a workforce we urgently need and who can still work, by contrast with the often-cited roofers or care workers who are physically exhausted. The newspaper headlines do them no favors.

Today hundreds of thousands are already working beyond retirement age, not necessarily for the money, but because they want to have a job that is about more than filling spare time or voluntary work. And I am convinced that this trend will continue. The reality has already outstripped some debates about misconceived justice.

Crucial to the question of whether we can continue to grow economically and maintain our social standards in future will be how quickly and sustainably we can progress digitalization. This is the mega-topic for the next few years and applies to all areas of our economy, such as driverless cars, health, or FinTech. We must endeavor to bring added digital value to Germany: this will then be immediately reflected in the federal budget through tax revenue.

When I talk about driverless cars at events I often get negative reactions. But we will all see this happen. And just as fifteen years ago many of us could not imagine ever using a cellphone and yet we do it every day today because it makes life easier, so it will be in other areas. Finally, we must—also with regard to the federal budget—highlight the issue of digital management. If we are honest, we have to admit that we in Germany are still in the digital Stone Age. If you change your place of residence, need a passport, or want to register your car, digitalization does not yet make much of an impact. Here we have to rethink massively and fundamentally—and very fast.

Of course, there is then the question of where the tax revenue comes from, if all services are digital and can be obtained from anywhere in the world. That is also important. But the real question is which processes are changing, how they are changing, and where value is added. For us, the focus should be on how we make management so efficient that money is not unnecessarily invested in structures that are already well on the way to being reproduced in completely different areas of life. So in the next four years we will need a minister of state to oversee this in the Chancellery. Every major organization is familiar with this: a particularly important topic is always a "matter for the boss."

These are by no means all the problems that will concern us in the future. One thing is certain, however: we want to manage the years to come as well without incurring new debt. Whether we can do that in the period leading up to 2030, I do not know. But every year we succeed gives us an enormous financial margin. In addition, the distribution of financial and tax resources in the country will be one of the biggest challenges of the future. We must do this together by 2030—even going beyond the compromises we have achieved in the financial equalization scheme between federal government and the regions. Here is the only place we can find the margin to finance the common good for the future. For the common good is expressed in nothing more than the figures and finances of a federal budget—that is as true today as it will be in 2030.

CHAPTER 6

THE LAW AS A FRAME OF REFERENCE FOR THE COMMON GOOD

CHRISTOPH G. PAULUS

Lawyers (including Pontius Pilate) know that there are insurmountable difficulties associated with a positive definition of justice, and that by contrast it is far easier to determine what is unjust. A similar aporia lies at the heart of this book's theme: even if everyone has a vague, rather unclear notion of what the common good means concretely—even in the 21st century—it is far easier to identify things that are detrimental to the common good and run counter to it. If these things are of a legal nature, that is determined by law, standards and legal provisions create a framework that influences the common good in whichever positive configuration and is thus of great influence and importance—an importance that is strengthened if this framework has an existence beyond the focus of general perception. In this case the frame of reference also has the potential to strangle the common good furtively and take ideas about it surreptitiously to absurd lengths.

Such a frame of reference will be the subject of this essay, namely the burden of debt on public finances, not only in Germany but, appallingly, almost across the entire world. The total amount has taken on dizzying proportions, and the feeling of dizziness is increased yet further if we try to follow how intensely the debt mountain grows each second on just one of the countless world debt clocks to be found on the Internet. The latest figures in the unbelievably long series of numbers (which in November 2017 came to a total of over 60 trillion dollars not counting the hidden debt) are not discernible, but represent just a flickering glimmer of an amount that is constantly growing with breathtaking speed.

Even if these shocking findings are in any way familiar, albeit usually placed in the box of what we like to repress about everyday life, the connection of this proliferating debt with the common good requires some explanation. In short, this connection consists for one thing in that debts imply power relationships, and for another thing they tie up resources that otherwise might perhaps be better used to promote the common good. In this essay, these two factors will be taken as premises, but not elaborated upon further. That subject needs to be pursued elsewhere.

In the first place, with regards to the power relationship existing between the creditor of a claim and their debtor, we must draw an initial distinction: debts as such are not bad and to be avoided. Rather, debts operate like many medicines: with the right dosage they can help, but given in excess they become poison. Where you draw the line in this obviously depends on countless factors as can be shown, for example, in the situation of the US, whose absolute record level of sovereign debt for a nation-state is regarded more as an expression of economic strength, while other states that have a fraction of its debt burden are listed as being on the verge of failure.

And yet, *grosso modo*, the equation still stands that a creditor has power over their debtor. We will not illustrate this here so much with reference to the global capital market, whose sheer extent (a multiple of global economic productivity) puts even such dominant institutions as the US Federal Reserve in the shade,[1] but rather through the example of the regular relationship in civil law between a borrower and a loan provider. Often this is a contract that law students encounter at the beginning of their studies. What we can learn here, among other things, is that a loan must be paid back at the end of an agreed period of time, so that this contractual relationship can then be placed *ad acta*: in legal terms, it can be extinguished. This simple regulation that, for example, is anchored in the German Civil Code (BGB; Section 362), but which can also be found in this or similar form in all private law statutes across the world, is never discussed in the context of the abovementioned astronomical sovereign debt burden. Thus in the case of said trillions, it is no longer a question of "fulfillment" and therefore the extinguishing of debt relationships, but clearly a question of something else. This something else brings us back to the question of power.

At the beginning of the contractual relationship, the borrower is free. Furthermore, every loan agreement contains the temptation to be able to carry out wishes today while the unpleasant part of the relationship, namely the repayment, lies in the more or less distant future. Psychologically, this factor should not be underestimated and it exerts a huge attraction. However, the closer the repayment and thus the unpleasant part of the relationship comes, the more the borrower (in Goethe's words) becomes a servant. This evolution from a free person to a servant has been intensified for some time now in the economic realm with the help of contractual clauses (known as covenants) that place a wealth of additional obligations on the borrower. These obligations are considered admissible because they serve the lender's need for protection, which is legitimate, or regarded as legitimate. Accordingly, one of the common goals of these clauses is simply to avoid the debtor's insolvency.

A consequence of the admissibility of such a procedure is that over the years these obligations accumulate and are fine-tuned more and more, and meanwhile the covenants are developed to such an extent that they leave the borrower only very limited room for their own initiative. If, on top of this, crisis indicators become acute, whether for external (exogenous) reasons or business (endogenous) reasons, the creditors' demonstration of power becomes apparent even to the outside world. This is usually the moment when consultants employed by the lender (the plural is used intentionally here, and refers not only to one creditor but to all where appropriate) more or less explicitly take over the management and thereby control of the company.

This is a development that is particularly important for our present context insofar as it is by no means limited to private law, but can be found in the public sphere as well. Here, however, information about the state of affairs is far more difficult to acquire and can often only be obtained indirectly. But such a conclusion regarding the shift in debtor-creditor power relations is very plain when one is made aware that these days China is increasingly making itself available as a lender to other states. For example, if Nigeria receives a loan of over 2 billion dollars, the aim is not the business that China can do in the shape of the interest it can pocket—this is of course merely the proverbial "peanuts" that no finance minister would ever be interested in. Much more important is that this "loan" commitment buys preferential access to this country's natural resources, such that this is (strictly speaking) a purchase contract according to the actual character of the agreement. And yet all the participants insist that the legal document is absolutely not to be characterized in this way, but rather as a loan agreement. The reason for this is that only through the (presumably *de facto* and by no means planned) possibility of demanding the loaned sum back can pressure be applied. It should also be mentioned that, in a legal insolvency context, classification as a loan or as a purchase contract is of huge importance, as completely different results ensue depending on which it is.

Against this backdrop, new insights also emerge, if we remember that once again it was China who, on the occasion of the Argentinian as well as the Greek crisis, very quickly announced publicly that it would be prepared to help out with loans. Once again we can exclude the idea that this was simply shrewd business behavior wanting to obtain new income opportunities in the shape of interest yields. Rather, the catalyst for this was the fact that the position of the creditor opens up opportunities of influence and thus enables a display of power. One consequence of these relationships is that for some time behind very closed doors work has been going on to focus loan agreements even more purposefully towards the increase of power. Typically, these efforts go by the (unsurprisingly warlike) name of "weaponization of financial instruments." For non-insiders, what this might look like in detail is currently the object of speculation at best.[2]

Nevertheless, it is at least clear that this is simply about acquiring influence that makes the use of weapons superfluous—for example in the way that aggregated demands can trigger the debtor nation's insolvency and thus social chaos (as for instance is still vividly demonstrated in Argentina or Greece). For example if—to name but one of several possible examples—health and elderly care collapse because doctors and nurses are left without salaries and medicines, there is no need to send in the tanks. All it needs is to offer medical care in return for capitulation, cession of territory, surrender of natural resources, or whatever else the desired objective may be.

After this proof of power as an implicit albeit highly present and dominant factor in loan relationships, if we now turn to the question of its connection with the common good, we should first of all remember the x trillion of public debt we mentioned at the outset, and also that it is not really a question of paying back these amounts but of paying off the interest. We do not need a great deal of mathematical knowledge to realize that even these amounts can reach huge proportions. In many countries on Earth (just under 40) it is this legal obligation to pay off just the interest that forces whole populations to live at or under subsistence level, making them what the International Monetary Fund (IMF) and the World Bank include under the acronym HIPC (High Indebted Poor Countries),[3] and subjecting them to a special debt repayment mechanism. But even for Germany and national budgets the ever-growing debt mountain means an ever-growing commitment to funds that then by definition cannot be spent or invested elsewhere, with the result that a not inconsiderable number of municipalities are *de facto* insolvent. For them, but also for a city such as New York, the question arises whether the streets might have been repaired a long time ago if the US's debt obligations were not devouring such horrendously large sums day in and day out.

Regardless of this mechanism, measures for the common good will still be introduced, at least in affluent countries. In any case, the capital needed to do this can be acquired regularly by means of newly procured funds, thus increasing the debt ratio—with the result that this leads to increased interest obligations, etc. etc.

In view of this, as it were, *perpetuum mobile* towards a virtually inevitable self-strangulation, it seems not unreasonable to cast around for alternative scenarios. These can engage with several points in the above problematic: for example with the absolutely compulsive search for ever more growth, or even with the question of whether one can, using a range of legal instruments, if not completely demolish the debt mountain then perhaps shrink it. The search for the latter range of instruments is an old one that can even be found in the Old Testament: Exodus (21:2), Deuteronomy (Chapter 15), and Leviticus

(25:8) describe the notion of the jubilee that offers a debt cancellation every 50 years. What seems like an ancient memory made waves once again less than 20 years ago: after Pope Boniface VIII had incorporated this Jewish tradition into Christianity in the year 1300, Pope John Paul II invoked it in his *Urbi et Orbi* address on January 1, 2000, calling for a general cancellation of debt for Third World countries. This appeal caused a furore in NGO circles across the world.

It is possible that the Pope created more than just a reaction among NGOs. For even if the Old Testament concept might be seen as a social utopia, Argentina's crisis, which was at that time becoming acute, nevertheless led to the IMF surprising the world with a suggestion for sovereign insolvency proceedings on the occasion of its 2001 fall meeting. At all events, an orderly legal process for debt reduction had previously been called for by NGOs, but had never reached the high political arena of multilateral organizations. This Sovereign Debt Restructuring Mechanism (SDRM) might even have been prompted by the papal address— the coincidence is at any rate striking.

Of course, the SDRM suggestion was not just about appealing to tradition and Christianity, but was rather an attempt to instrumentalize mechanisms that were already legally available in the form of insolvency proceedings. In any case, the IMF's efforts did not meet with success, at least not direct success. The political determination did not exist. Even the massive and unbelievably high-profile[4] crisis in Greece did not manage to change politicians' minds—even though some completely understood the need for action. The significant advantage of such a procedure would ultimately have been to control the debt burden in a structured, orderly way, thus liberating it from the unpredictable exercise of power and political opportunism. This would have been at least one of the ways of solving the tangible drama of global debt problems, not as before through the accumulation of more debt, but by reducing it. The freed-up payment obligations could then form at least the basis (if not the guarantee) for creating the common good, particularly for the 21st century.

Alongside these findings—findings that provide little cause for optimism—there are still isolated oases of hope at the political level. At the moment there are essentially only individuals, and some individual countries, who are looking increasingly for appropriate solutions. Among the latter, Singapore stands out: it has for some time been devoting due attention and great concern to the debt ratio, and as a consequence in July 2017 contractually agreed to set up a subsidiary of the

Permanent Court of Arbitration which had hitherto only existed in The Hague. In this institution, which started work at the beginning of 2018, Singapore has already proposed to trial the setting up of a Sovereign Debt Tribunal, in order to create a kind of court of state insolvency. What might be achieved by this is currently still the subject of much debate and discussion. But such a "court" might offer the foundation and a forum for bringing debtor countries together with their creditors at negotiations, which follow a procedure that is specified and on occasion supervised by the "judges," and which has to produce results after a period of perhaps two years, results which will then be judged. Such a structured approach would have invaluable benefits, not the least of which would lie in the finance minister, prime minister, or other responsible person being given instructions for handling a situation that in all probability they had never hitherto experienced, let alone got to grips with.

Singapore's venture is not the first attempt in this direction: similar expressions of interest existed earlier on (coming, for example, from Russia around 120 years ago and from Liechtenstein just a few years ago). What had hitherto failed does not have to remain so for all time. It is possible that in our time the legal foundations can be established whereby a suitable frame of reference for the common good of the future will be created.

Notes

1. Cf. Heike Buchter in *Die Zeit*, November 2, 2017.

2. Cf. Christoph G. Paulus, "Schritte auf dem Weg zu einem Resolvenzrecht für zahlungsunfähige Staaten" in *Wertpapier-Mitteilungen*, issue 20 (2015), p. 953 ff.

3. On the debt relief initiatives of the World Bank and the IMF for these countries in particular, see: http://web.worldbank.org/WBSITE/EXTERNAL/TOPICS/EXTDEBTDEPT/0,,contentMDK:20655535~menuPK:64166739~page PK:64166689~piPK:64166646~theSitePK:469043,00.html (accessed November 20, 2017).

4. The deeply troubling antithesis to the public nature of the Greek tragedy is the current and ongoing sovereign bank-ruptcies of virtually all the island states in the South Seas and the Caribbean. The fact that global warming is forcing them constantly and increasingly to spend more to save their coasts, driving them further and further into ruin is not, as far as we can see, worth reporting by the news media.

CHAPTER 7

GLOBAL SUSTAINABILITY AS A GOAL OF THE COMMON GOOD

STEFAN KORIOTH

I.

In 1972, a report on "the limits to growth," commissioned by the Club of Rome, an independent, interdisciplinary group of experts, was published. The study, which for the first time outlined not only mathematical and statistical but also computer-aided future scenarios, had been written by a group of authors from the Massachusetts Institute of Technology. In order to predict the limits of the planet's further development in various projections, the researchers initially utilized two conventional factors whose combined effect had already received some attention in the 19th century, namely global population growth and food production. Taking other factors into account, the report went on to break new ground. It attempted to measure the extent and growth of what was then called "degradation of the environment," and also to measure both the reserves of non-renewable resources and industrial output. The result of the interaction of these five factors, mathematically underpinned in their calculations by the System Dynamics method, was an apocalyptic vision of the future. The absolute limits of growth on Earth would be reached by around 2070 if the increases in global population, degradation of the environment, industrial output, and consumption of natural resources, as identified in 1972, continued unchanged. In such a case, the report said, there would be a risk of collapse in the environment, the industrial sector, and the service sector with unforeseeable consequences for human civilization. Immediate and effective counter-measures were required. The report suggested achieving this through a particular state of equilibrium, using growth limitations in all areas within industrialized countries (compulsory if necessary), and controlled growth of agriculture and industry in Third World countries.

The report met with overwhelming acclaim, sold millions in book form, and in Germany was stocked by all high-quality bookstores, which piled it high next to the checkout. After many isolated attempts during the 1960s, *The Limits to Growth* provided the initial impetus for the global environmental movement. This indeed was its fundamental contribution. Ever since, no one can deny that the meticulously detailed problems are vital questions for humanity, that is, questions concerning the common good as such. However, the report also contained lots of questionable aspects (more easily identifiable in retrospect than they were in 1972) that were passed on to the environmental movement and that in part persist today. In the first place, it was the technocratic approach that immediately recommended control and coercion, for example in the case of population growth in order to limit the size of the subsequent generation. In addition, ecology and economics were played off against each other in a rather crude way, with economic growth classed as potentially dangerous—the notion that growth can also have potential for improved environmental protection and more careful use of resources[1] was not explicitly rejected, but equally was not taken into consideration.

Ultimately, what is striking from today's perspective is that the problems were indeed identified and described as global challenges, but the possible solutions were associated equally self-evidently with limited collective bodies: societies, nations, and states. This could be seen most clearly in the Club of Rome's stated goal (which no one questions as such) of improving the welfare of the hitherto underprivileged and their societies, while conversely enforcing a concept of sacrifice in developed countries.

Theoretical debate went beyond this limited perspective in the 1980s[2]—while the Club of Rome's 1972 report remained relevant in this context by updating its own work. In the decade that saw the Chernobyl disaster and that ended with the fall of the Berlin Wall and the hope of a world without ideological differences, it was recognized that hitherto humanity had debated all questions of the common good—whatever was understood by this concept—with three limitations that should be challenged: a temporal limitation—the common good refers to the present and at most the near future; a regional viewpoint that was typically focused on states; and third and last, a viewpoint that concentrates on limited groups and collective bodies with a sense of solidarity, and that distinguishes one group from all others and champions internal altruism as well as (moderate or unchecked) egotism with regard to all other groups. The fact that environment- and development-related questions shatter these three limitations was an insight that was as obvious as it was new. This new situation was immediately given a positive slant, particularly by contrast with the rather gloomy atmosphere of the 1970s. This was certainly the case in high-flying theories and their subsequent proclamations. The new buzzword in this unlimited, more comprehensive, and positive kind of thinking was global sustainability of development in a "one world" society. The 1987 Brundtland Report, *Our Common Future*,[3] recommended future-proof, sustainable development in a triangle of the most diverse goals that are to be achieved as broadly as possible both simultaneously and in parallel. According to the report, the ecological goals should take into account that human civilizations would have to adapt to the limited carrying capacity of the Earth's eco-system, in particular the limits of non-renewable resources. In the case of economic goals, the report continues, it is a question of maintaining production capital including the Earth's natural capital. Wherever possible, there must be a conversion from consumption to a recycling economy. Social goals require basic human needs to be met everywhere in the world. Transcending all limits, this was nothing less than the proclamation of a global society of solidarity and justice, bound to the common good, which had hitherto been regarded as utopian. "What is required is a new approach in which all nations aim at a type of development that integrates production with resource conservation and enhancement, and that links both to the provision for all of an adequate livelihood base and equitable access to resources."[4] And: "Sustainable development involves more than growth. It requires a change in the context of growth, to make it less material- and energy-intensive and more equitable in its impact."[5]

II.

In the three decades that followed, the law became suffused with this concept of sustainability at all levels—in international law, in European Union law, and in national legal systems. Here in particular is where we find the reason behind the increasing use of objective-oriented programs in legal provisions— the designation of goals and target coordinates to be achieved as far as possible, instead of conditional programs of fixed conditions and legal consequences. For instance, there are two examples of the positively inflationary use of the sustainability principle. In the Preamble to the Treaty on European Union (2007 version), the EU declares it is "determined to promote economic and social progress for their peoples, taking into account the principle of sustainable development and within the context of the accomplishment of the internal market and of reinforced cohesion and environmental protection, and to implement policies ensuring that advances in economic integration are accompanied by parallel progress in other fields." This is concretized in individual areas of activity. German environmental law is full of sustainability obligations. In Section 1(5) of the Federal Building Code, construction planning law demands that "land-use plans shall safeguard sustainable urban development and a socially equitable utilization of land for the general good of the community." Urban land-use plans should "contribute to securing a more humane environment and to protecting and developing the basic conditions for natural life. ..." The inflationary conjuring of the concept of sustainability, sometimes in general terms, sometimes in specific areas, can be seen in many other examples. And yet, even 30 years after the 1987 Brundtland Report, the concept of concretizing the common good through recourse to the concept of sustainability seems remarkably hollow and thin.

Its outcomes and impacts become weaker the more they want to influence a limitless and future-oriented global society, or at any rate the fate of the world. Now as then, thinking in global contexts is hard, and the law regularly gets tangled up when doing so. But why, even in 2017, do our notions of justice and the common good concern themselves so stubbornly (and thus perhaps also justifiably) with the system of groups living at the same time and in the same place, from the family to the nation, using the juxtapositions of inclusion and exclusion, today and tomorrow, inward-looking altruism and outward-looking egotism?

First, this surely goes hand in hand with a solid, fundamental anthropological configuration. Manageability enables shaping and acting. Freedom, equality, and responsibility can flourish in action and reaction, in personal involvement and supervision. For Aristotle, the common good was the good of the manageable *polis*; if certain conditions are met, Rousseau's social contract constituted the common good as expressed by the general will by contrast with the totality of individual wills—but only for the contracting parties.[6] Today, anyone dealing with a wider context enters a harmonious world of abstraction that can often, however, scarcely construct relationships of responsibility any more. "In this view of things," writes Meinhard Miegel, "even the Earth, Nature, and the Universe themselves are held in the bosom of the common good. The fact that both the concept of freedom and of the common good [...] are no longer practicable as a result of this, seems to arouse little concern."[7] Western European values may appear to claim general validity and universality, but since antiquity their mode of realization has been the city-state, and now the nation-state. In practice, the dominant idea is that the world can be improved through work and the clever application of economic and technological means—an idea that is also religiously underpinned, despite everyone being created in the image of God in Christianity. Europe entered its phase of technical and military superiority over other regions of the globe (a superiority that was in part deployed brutally for its own ends), when it subdivided into nations that are in competition with each other.

Moreover, particular power resides in the individual- and group-related idea that the common good might develop (of itself if the basic conditions of honesty and fairmindedness are met) if each individual looks out for their own benefit and that of their neighbors, and thus enters into extensive relationships of exchange with everyone else, which are to the benefit of all. Thus the baker might best contribute to the common good by selling decent bread at reasonable prices, paying taxes on his earnings, and providing for his family. This view also reminds us that we always talk about the common good as individuals first. Anyone invoking abstract, supra-individual values as the common good, in the name of any idea whatsoever, is reliant on particular justifying requirements. This is how we should understand the words of Carl Schmitt, when he said that anyone who speaks of the *bonum commune* is intent on deception. Political rhetoric frequently has recourse "to the argument of the common good in order to procure a moral advantage over the weight of expertise, and to cut short the debate. Herein lies the temptation for authorities, who want to avoid justification, to decree what the common good demands with the result that 'common good' becomes a synonym for 'end of discussion'."[8]

Ultimately, there are two proven organizational principles related to the common good that refer categorically to the manageable organization and its advantages: these are the principles of decentralization and subsidiarity. For example, according to Germany's Basic Law [*Grundgesetz*], federalism in the form of the federal structure and the protection of municipal self-government along with the manageability of the local community (Article 28[2] Basic Law) play a particular role especially in the realization of the principle of democracy and thus of the common good. The smaller entity is thought to have a special capacity for problem-solving, the municipality is considered the nucleus of democracy, and here citizen engagement related to the common good has a range of deployment that is protected from interventions from above. The principle of subsidiarity itself demands that in a vertically structured organization a task be assigned to the smaller entity wherever possible. This primacy of the smaller entity is evoked by Article 5(3) of the Treaty on European Union in the form of a demand which serves more to appease the Member States, however, than as a demonstration of concrete substance: "Under the principle of subsidiarity, in areas which do not fall within its exclusive competence, the Union shall act only if and in so far as the objectives of the proposed action cannot be sufficiently achieved by the Member States, either at central level or at regional and local level, but can rather, by reason of the scale or effects of the proposed action, be better achieved at Union level."

The patterns of thought and conflict resolution in the manageable entity are thus alive and powerful, frequently with the best reasons and results, while concern for the sustainable, global common good has only limited chances of being realized if it relies directly upon cooperation at global level—in spite of everything we know about the global nature of environmental and peace problems. This can sometimes lead to remarkable amalgamations of levels and to exaggerations. Germany's withdrawal from nuclear energy, which was announced overnight in March 2011, was justified on the basis of global considerations, as if Germany, acting on behalf of or leading the whole world, could condemn the peaceful use of nuclear energy. Oddly enough, the fact that nuclear power plants continue to produce electricity in all Germany's neighbors, except Denmark and Austria, and new plants are even being planned and built, did not trouble the debate in Germany. And, what is Trump's "America First" slogan if not a crude attempt to revert to the state as the sole administrator of the common good, when this simply does not work in the face of international interdependencies in environmental protection and trade relationships? In a completely counterfactual way, a pamphlet written by advisors to the US President intends to show that for the US no international goals of the common good can exist outside its own borders. Being "masters of the universe," it claims, could only damage the US. Equally, the Brexit decision can be seen as an expression of the desire to seek the common good in the manageable community alone, and to refuse everything that does not originate in the United Kingdom.

III.

If this is the case, however, if the difficulty of negotiating and deciding questions pertaining to the common good globally cannot be overcome, and if in practice sustainability and the common good are concentrated in manageable groups and time periods, what is to be done? Cosmopolitan rhetoric is of little help in such a case, and the problems must be solved piecemeal in the location where they can be solved. As Timo Meynhardt writes: "In this case the common good would be appreciable for individuals most of all when the quality of coexistence in a social collective is put to the test, when disruptions occur in such a system, or previous experiences are placed in doubt. The crux of the matter is always the perceiving, evaluating, and interpreting individual."[9] This can be illustrated by some examples. Aspects of sustainability with reference to the common good in the form of intergenerational justice play a particular role in issues of social security, national debt, and environmental protection. As safeguarding against life crises (poverty in old age, illness, unemployment) through insurance and more generally through the welfare state relies on give and take, redistribution, autonomy, and solidarity, only national solutions are conceivable. The same applies to national debt—in this case all European attempts to establish solidarity or a community of liability between states lead inevitably to upheavals, false incentives, and backlashes. Equally, actions taken to protect the environment have the greatest chance of success in the national context. Putting a price on the use of scarce environmental resources, and thereby limiting this use as far as possible, can best succeed within a manageable organization, despite the global nature of the things we want to protect. Indeed, environmental levies require a regulating, parliamentary authority and transparency when it comes to charging the levy and value for money. This points to the state as the arena for such development. At the same time, in the case of globally operating companies, the asymmetry is clear. Eco-taxes can lead to taxed companies relocating to other countries.

Lastly, let us look at another area that raises questions of sustainability with regard to the common good, namely the flow of migration over the last few years and the consequent European refugee crisis that can only be resolved by transnational action, which does not even occur within the European regulatory framework. The legal regulatory framework provided by the EU to deal with this problem is clear: the combined effect of "Dublin III" and the concept of safe third states (see Basic Law Article 16a) provided by individual nations' laws concentrates the problem on the EU states located at the outer limits of the EU, and produces considerable trends towards disintegration. In this framework, the Member State first entered by an asylum seeker is responsible for the asylum procedure within the EU. For the northern Member States, including Germany, which is surrounded by safe third states, this means that only people who have entered Germany directly from a non-EU country by sea or air (a rare occurrence) can claim asylum in Germany. As we know, things are very different in practice, as a wave of refugees comprising a million people cannot be dealt with in this way. This is nothing less than the rediscovery of the nation-state as a frame of reference for problem-solving, and a further challenge to the attempt to resolve questions concerning the common good transnationally and internationally. Nevertheless, our consciousness and the state of our knowledge have transcended the boundaries into modernity: "But what might be called a society's 'threshold of modernity' has been reached when the life of the species is wagered on its own political strategies. For millennia, man remained what he was for Aristotle: a living animal with an additional capacity for a political existence; modern man is an animal whose politics places his existence as a living being in question."[10]

Notes

1. It was observed very early on that from a certain point rising per capita income very often went hand in hand with declining air and water pollution. Cf. Mathias Binswanger, "Sustainable Development: Utopie in einer wachsenden Wirtschaft?" in *Zeitschrift für Umweltpolitik und Umweltrecht*, vol. 1 (1995), p. 1 ff.

2. See importantly: Hans Jonas, *The Imperative of Responsibility: In Search of an Ethics for the Technological Age* (Chicago: University of Chicago Press, 1984).

3. World Commission on Environment and Development (WCED), *Our Common Future* (Oxford: Oxford University Press, 1987).

4. Op. cit., p. 39 ff.

5. Op. cit., p. 52.

6. Immanuel Kant, too, in *Perpetual Peace: A Philosophical Sketch* (1795), subscribed to this idea, but alongside the notion of constitutional law, he also looked at international law and the conditions and possibilities of a "law of world citizenship" (Third Definitive Article).

7. Meinhard Miegel, "Freiheit und Gemeinwohl: Eine sozial-
   wissenschaftliche Perspektive" in *Freiheit und Gemeinwohl*
   ed. by Hans-Jürgen Papier and Timo Meynhardt (Hamburg:
   Tempus Corporate, 2016), pp. 87 ff., 89 f.

8. Josef Isensee, "Was heißt Gemeinwohl? Zu Begriff, Idee
   und praktischer Relevanz" in Isensee, op. cit., pp. 37 ff., 43,
   including the Schmitt reference.

9. Timo Meynhardt, "Ohne Gemeinwohl keine Freiheit: Zur
   Psychologie des Gemeinwohls" in op. cit., pp. 173 ff., 190.

10. Michel Foucault, *The Will to Knowledge: The History of
    Sexuality*, trans. Robert Hurley, vol. 1 (London: Penguin,
    1998), p. 143.

CHAPTER 8

GLOBAL HEALTH—PART OF THE COMMON GOOD OR A PRIVATE COMMODITY?

STEFAN OSCHMANN

Right this second, scientists and entrepreneurs all over the world and venture capitalists in Silicon Valley and elsewhere are working to defeat death. Start-ups dedicated to fighting the aging process and extending human life attract large amounts of capital.[1] New technologies such as genome editing with CRISPR allow scientists to take an engineering approach to biology. Digitization and big data analysis further accelerate the scientific process. Ray Kurzweil, futurist and Google's Director of Engineering, even predicts that by 2050, we will walk into a doctor's office and receive a make-over treatment every few years.[2]

Will death soon be optional? In the end, this question is secondary. Something else is much more important. The dynamics we are currently witnessing in science and technology are fundamentally changing health care.

For a very long time, health care's sole purpose was to tend to the sick and dying. It was meant to alleviate pain and suffering. From ancient Egypt and Greece to medieval Europe, health care was closely linked to religious institutions. As science progressed, products and services became more differentiated. What once was charity evolved into a thriving industry. Today, health care accounts for more than 10 percent of GDP in advanced economies.[3]

Treating and curing patients still is health care's major task. But scientific progress and digital technologies increasingly enable patients to take matters into their own hands. Just consider the thousands and thousands of health apps we can install on our smartphones to analyze personal health data; or how new services such as genome sequencing make it possible to assess our personal risk of developing certain diseases. In light of these developments, one question arises: is health still part of what we refer to as the "common good" or is it becoming a private commodity?

Let us look at this question from a practitioner's perspective. The concept of the common good has been widely discussed in philosophy and social theory since the days of Plato and Aristotle. A rather general definition refers to the common good as the maximum well-being of a society. If we accept the notion of the common good, further questions come to mind: how can we specify it? Can we define it at all? Philosophically, I share Karl Popper's view that there is no such thing as a final historic state towards which society evolves. Consequently, there can be no final, objective definition of what constitutes the common good. Instead of pursuing a grand vision, we should take pragmatic steps and seek incremental improvements to specific problems.

In the health field, we have made remarkable progress in recent years:

- Between 2000 and 2015, global average life expectancy increased by five years—the fastest increase since the 1960s.

- The maternal mortality ratio has declined by 45 percent worldwide since 1990.

125

• The number of new HIV infections dropped by 40 percent between 2000 and 2013 and deaths halved.

Yet we have also learned that health crises have serious negative consequences, for example when it comes to economics. Diseases harm economic growth and development. In Europe, cancer leads to lost productivity of more than 50 billion euros—every single year. Diseases also pose a threat to flourishing trade and the stability of financial markets. Just think of the global scare caused by the SARS epidemic in southern China back in 2003. Health can even affect the social stability of entire countries and regions. This was obvious during the Ebola crisis in West Africa three years ago. It is therefore no surprise that health has a firm place on the agenda of high-caliber policy meetings such as the Munich Security Conference.

In light of these developments, one aspect becomes clear: the best way to ensure our own health is to be concerned about the health of everyone else. Fostering global health means fostering the common good. So, yes, health is part of the common good. And it will remain so in the future.

The health challenges we currently face as a global community are severe:

- Non-communicable diseases such as cancer, diabetes, and cardiovascular diseases are on the rise around the globe. They kill almost 40 million people every year.[4]

- Antimicrobial resistance, or AMR, is a major public health threat. These days, 700,000 people die each year due to AMR.[5] By the year 2050, that number could rise to a staggering 10 million.[6]

- The so-called "neglected" tropical diseases such as Chagas, Guinea worm disease, or schistosomiasis plague about one billion people. Often they affect the poorest of the poor in developing countries.

There is no one-size-fits-all solution to these health hazards. We need different approaches. First and foremost, there are scientific challenges we must deal with. Consider the case of cancer. Over the past few years, immunotherapies have brought great progress. These new medicines seek to activate the immune system to fight cancer. They offer the chance of a cure to a considerable number of patients. But for a greater portion of patients, they are not effective. And we do not yet know why. Therefore, we need to develop further therapies. And the most promising way to do so is through our current system of innovation: competitive research, strong intellectual property rights, and rewards for the successful innovator. Or to put it differently: to ultimately foster the common good, innovation must have the characteristics of a private good.

Our current system of innovation has become the target of substantial criticism. Critics argue that strong intellectual property protection prevents access to treatment for many. Consequently, some propose rewarding successful innovation with predefined sums of money that more or less reflect the development cost plus a certain premium, for example, x euros for the development of a new cancer treatment. Intellectual property would then be openly accessible and any drug company could produce the medicine. According to this view, patients would benefit from lower prices.

Others propose fully public tax-financed medicines. This is in part constructive criticism worth debating. But in my opinion, these cost-based approaches are not suitable options in most cases for several reasons. First, considering research and development costs alone is too simplistic. Biopharmaceutical medicines reduce overall health care costs, for example by lowering spending on hospitalization. And they enable patients to work and remain productive members of society for longer. Rather than input costs, the value of medicines should reflect this societal benefit.

Second, to treat effectively diseases such as cancer or Alzheimer's, we need further breakthrough innovation. But for breakthrough innovation to happen, the potential reward must compensate the innovator for the risk of failure. This risk is very high in pharmaceutical research. Only 12 percent of the drug candidates that enter clinical trials receive approval for use in patients;[7] 88 percent fail—almost 9 out of 10. If potential rewards more or less reflected the input costs, what company would take this kind of a risk? The industry would pursue a much less riskier path. Research would focus on areas with a high probability of success. I do not think this would be a desirable outcome.

The current system of innovation based on competitive research, strong intellectual property rights, and rewards for the successful innovator is our best option to meet most of the scientific challenges we face. It helps us to create, improve, and prolong lives. It supports us in developing new technologies that accelerate access to better health for everyone.

This does not mean that the current system is perfect—for health care and the entire economy. Sebastian Buckup, a researcher at the World Economic

Forum, argues that the economic policies of recent decades paired with technological progress have led to an increasing concentration of power in the hands of just a few players, namely within the financial and technology industries. This concentration allows firms to hoard profits and invest less. In Buckup's view, policymakers must come up with new approaches. He makes one important point that I share: he emphasizes that a vibrant entrepreneurial ecosystem is the most effective antidote to the concentration of economic power. It should therefore be easier for start-ups to scale up quickly. Economic rules should incentivize value creation over value capture. This is critical. If we want to seize the potential of science and technology, we need the right economic rules in place. And the debate over how such rules should be shaped is, in my view, critical for our future economic success.

The current system of innovation drives forward the development of many new medicines. Yet there is one area where it utterly fails—antimicrobial resistance. Everyone agrees that we need new antibiotics as medicines of last resort. Yet we are struggling with the development of new medicines. Why?

The idea of new antibiotics is to use them only when all other medicines fail. Ideally, they are not to be used at all. And just as it is impossible to recruit soldiers if they are paid by the shots they eventually fire, it is impossible to expect companies to invest billions into the development of drugs for which there is ideally very little demand. To tackle antimicrobial resistance, we need alternative incentive models.

We must deal with scientific challenges. But at the same time, we must mind the ethical aspects of global health, because health affects individuals' well-being in the most fundamental manner possible. The distribution of health care immediately raises questions of equity, fairness, and dignity.

One point is very important to me in this respect. We should not discuss ethical aspects solely in terms of redistribution. Instead, we should bear in mind what the philosopher Harry G. Frankfurt emphasized regarding equality:

> Economic equality is not, as such, of any particular moral importance; and by the same token, economic inequality is not in itself morally objectionable. From the point of view of morality, it is not important that everyone should have *the same*. What is morally important is that each should have *enough*.[8]

Or to put it differently: it is morally important that everyone has access to effective health care. And this is not the case by far! For example, non-communicable diseases such as cancer, cardiovascular disease, diabetes, and many more are often referred to as diseases of affluence. But that is not true. Actually, developing countries bear the brunt of the burden. Three out of four deaths due to non-communicable diseases occur there.[9]

Many health care systems in these countries are completely ill-equipped to cope with the burden of these plagues. Imagine a cancer patient in Africa. Most likely, they will be diagnosed too late. They hardly have access to modern health care services. Often, they even lack basic painkillers. And even when they receive treatment, chances are high that they will have to pay for it out of their own pocket. Disease not only ruins health, it also ruins finances. We cannot accept such circumstances.

An important approach to improving access to health is inter-sectoral partnerships beyond traditional ideological barriers. Many joint initiatives between public institutions, civil society organizations, and the private sector have proven to be very effective. They have led to significant achievements, for example in the fight against HIV/AIDS or malaria and neglected tropical diseases.

We need more of this. The challenges we face when it comes to non-communicable diseases are too great and too complex for any one group to tackle alone.

I firmly believe that if we collaborate across sectors, we can significantly improve patients' lives in low- and middle- income countries. We can improve the common good.

At the 2017 Davos World Economic Forum, 22 biopharmaceutical companies, together with the World Bank and the Union for International Cancer Control, launched Access Accelerated. This is the first cross-sectoral partnership to improve the care for non-communicable diseases in developing countries. Many companies are already doing a lot in this area. Now, private industry is joining forces with public institutions and civil society organizations. Together, we are going to address the broad range of barriers to better care, including aspects such as financing and regulatory harmonization.

Access Accelerated shows that the private sector has a lot to contribute. Of course, this partnership is not the only answer to the challenge posed by non-communicable diseases. The global community at large can and should do much more to address this issue. The global community can and should do more to improve global health and work towards the common good.

Let me refer to my initial question: is health still a part of what we call the common good or is it becoming a private commodity? Is it preferable to socialize health fully or to privatize it fully?

Actually, both are true. Health is and will remain part of the common good. But for innovation to thrive, we depend on health care products and services being developed by private players. And we need the private sector to lean in to work towards equitable access to health. Striving towards the common good will always involve conflict between various interest groups. And this is a good thing. It touches on what, in my opinion, is the most important aspect regarding the common good in the 21st century: we must come out of our trenches and put ideological differences aside. We can agree to disagree on certain topics and still work together to improve global health. This might not sound very exciting. But it has proven to be highly effective.

It gives us reason to look optimistically to the future. Or to put it in the words of Nelson Mandela: "Where people of goodwill get together and transcend their differences for the common good, peaceful and just solutions can be found even for those problems which seem most intractable."[10]

This article is based on a speech given by Stefan Oschmann on July 29, 2017, as part of the Convoco Forum in Salzburg.

Notes

1. https://www.scientificamerican.com/article/radical-life-extension-is-not-around-the-corner (accessed November 8, 2017).

2. Yuval Noah Harari, *Homo Deus: A Brief History of Tomorrow* (New York: Vintage, 2017), p. 25; http://www.newyorker.com/magazine/2017/04/03/silicon-valleys-quest-to-live-forever (accessed November 8, 2017).

3. http://data.worldbank.org/indicator/SH.XPD.TOTL.ZS (accessed November 8, 2017).

4. https://ncdalliance.org (accessed November 8, 2017).

5. https://ec.europa.eu/health/amr/antimicrobial-resistance_en (accessed November 8, 2017).

6. https://www.ifpma.org/resource-centre/new-alliance-to-drive-and-measure-industry-progress-to-curb- antimicrobial-resistance (accessed November 8, 2017).

7. http://phrma-docs.phrma.org/files/dmfile/Prescription-Medicines---Costs-in-Context---June-2017.pdf, p. 22 (accessed November 8, 2017).

8. Harry G. Frankfurt, *On Inequality* (Princeton, NJ: Princeton University Press, 2015), p. 7.

9. https://ncdalliance.org/why-ncds/NCDs_Sustainable_Human_Development (accessed November 8, 2017).

10. http://www.mandela.gov.za/mandela_speeches/1999/990128_medienpreis.htm (accessed November 8, 2017).

CHAPTER 9

TO WHAT EXTENT SHOULD THE ENTREPRENEUR FOCUS ON THE COMMON GOOD?

KAI A. KONRAD

In the past few years, the market economy system has been subject to criticism, and with it the profit-orientated entrepreneur. For example, Susanne Schmidt won the 2010 *Wirtschaftsbuchpreis* [Economic Book Prize] for her book on the crisis in the financial markets, titled *Markt ohne Moral: Das Versagen der Finanzelite* [*Markets without Morality: The Failure of the Financial Elite*].[1] And on Amazon's trading platform, Cardinal Reinhard Marx's book, *Das Kapital: Ein Plädoyer für den Menschen* [*Capital: A Plea for Humanity*] is promoted using this quote from the author: "Capitalism without humanity, solidarity, and justice has no morality and also no future."[2] In public debate, there is a rush to pillory the greed of managers and entrepreneurs. In the same vein, investigative journalism is making an impact with the Panama Papers and numerous press reports.

In the movie world, too, the topic of "greed" has been addressed, resulting in the creation of some brilliant masterpieces. The 2011 movie *Margin Call*, by director and screenwriter J.C. Chandor, highlights in telling fashion the greed- and fear-driven activities and decision-making processes in a large, fictional, financial trading company on Wall Street on the eve of the financial crisis. Oliver Stone's classic 1987 film *Wall Street* depicts the character of finance shark Gordon Gekko, played by Michael Douglas, who wants to make substantial profits by taking over and asset-stripping Teldar Paper, a fictional company. At the company's crucial shareholders' meeting, he gives a remarkable speech, which includes the following passage:

> The point is, ladies and gentlemen, that greed, for lack of a better word, is good. Greed is right, greed works. Greed clarifies, cuts through, and captures the essence of the evolutionary spirit. Greed, in all of its forms; greed for life, for money, for love, knowledge

has marked the upward surge of mankind. And greed, you mark my words, will not only save Teldar Paper, but that other malfunctioning corporation called the USA. Thank you very much.[3]

Gordon Gekko is the "villain" of the movie. He seduces the shareholders, arousing their primeval instincts and manipulating them. In Gordon Gekko's hymn to greed, the film is actually quoting Ivan Boesky, an important business partner of Michael Milken, who was later prosecuted by the US authorities for financial fraud.[4] On May 18, 1986, Boesky is reported to have said in a speech to business studies students at the University of California, Berkeley: "Greed is all right, by the way. I want you to know that. I think greed is healthy. You can be greedy and still feel good about yourself."[5]

Gordon Gekko's statement, however, is of far greater import. He is not concerned with feelings of guilt. Rather, Gekko's argument leads us to a really central question. Let us assume that the focus on self-interest is a central driving force in human behavior: what are the consequences for society and the economy, and for entrepreneurial behavior?

Economic theory has a surprising answer to this question. In rudimentary form, the answer goes back as far as Adam Smith, the father of the economic sciences. In his book, *An Inquiry into the Nature and Causes of the Wealth of Nations*, we find the following:

> As every individual, therefore, endeavors as much as he can both to employ his capital in the support of domestic industry, and so to direct that industry that its produce may be of the greatest value; every individual necessarily labors to render the annual revenue of the society as great as he can. He generally, indeed, neither intends to promote the public interest, nor knows how much he is promoting it. By preferring the support of domestic to that of foreign industry, he intends only his own security; and by directing that industry in such a manner as its produce may be of the greatest value, he intends only his own gain, and he is in this, as in many other cases, led by an invisible hand to promote an end which was no part of his intention.[6]

The entrepreneur who wants only to maximize their profit thus contributes in the maximum way possible to the prosperity of society precisely through the one-sided focus of their activity on their own profit. How can that be? The key to understanding this lies in the often misunderstood nature of production and trade. A customer only buys a product for a given price if the price is no higher than the maximum the buyer would be prepared to pay for it. Thus it is typically the case that the majority of those buying the product would have been quite prepared to accept an even higher price. They thus benefit as a result of their purchase. And the seller is only prepared to sell the product at this price, if the price compensates them at least for the expenses and costs they have incurred. Voluntary trading at a market-clearing price thus ensures that both sides of the market, seller and buyer, benefit from the exchange of goods for money, or money for goods. Trade is typically not a zero-sum game in which one side can only win what the other side loses. Rather, exchange offers both trading partners a real advantage. A competitive economic market is an institution that perfects this kind of commercial activity.

Some 200 years later, economic theory, in particular general equilibrium theory, has taken a fresh look at the ideas of Adam Smith. One of the most important thinkers in this area, the Nobel Laureate Gérard Debreu, is credited with clarifying this topic in the two "Fundamental Theorems of Welfare Economics."[7] The first fundamental principle describes the quality of the production, trading, and consumption activities that result from an economic system that is perfectly organized as a competitive market: in a "model" form of capitalism, with competitive economic markets and normal production conditions, the economic activity is "optimal" in an important sense. It is a situation that cannot be improved by state intervention. All opportunities for increasing welfare universally have been exhausted. State intervention can only redistribute: any improvement in the conditions of one person or group necessarily leads to the disadvantage of other people or groups.

Debreu's findings initially leave questions of distributive justice open. Even very extreme situations, in which a few people own almost everything while everyone else owns almost nothing, would be "optimal" according to Debreu. These might be situations in which the fate of the "have-nots" would only improve at the expense of the "haves." Debreu addresses the question of the distributive justice of market economies in the second Fundamental Theorem of Welfare Economics. He comes to the following conclusion: whatever the standards of a society appear to be in questions of distributive justice, one can reach an outcome that fully implements these standards by appropriately redistributing the initial assets of the members of the society. However, once property rights and starting opportunities are defined in this way, then the driving forces of self-interested trade in competitive economic markets should be allowed to take over. The mechanisms of a competitive market economy do not only reach an efficient outcome, but also become the agents of welfare and distribution objectives in society.

Thus, under certain conditions of market-economic activity, Gordon Gekko's argument is not wrong. And Debreu's observations also perhaps form the basis of the answer Nobel Laureate Milton Friedman gave to the question of the true purpose of business, namely that the social responsibility of business is to increase its own profits.[8]

Recent events might cause many people to regard Debreu's conclusions and Milton Friedman's words as cynical provocations. In 2007, the business practices of the financial sector led to a serious financial crisis, in which the collateral damage was enormous, in addition affecting people who had nothing to do with the financial sector. Investment banks and insurance companies had entered into investment risks that far surpassed their own means to compensate for possible losses. When losses occurred, they could not for the most part bear them themselves. And this meant that uninvolved third parties had to bear the losses, the taxpayer most of all.

There can be no doubt that the behaviors and mechanisms that led to the financial crisis caused major welfare losses. So were Adam Smith, Gérard Debreu, and Milton Friedman wrong? And are the critics of the "market" and of "capitalism" right? Does unbridled self-interest really not lead to good results? Should we simply prescribe a "dose of morals" to the investment banks involved in the financial crisis and the CFOs of major international corporations, inject them with a greater sense of social responsibility, and demand their commitment to social welfare objectives?

Anyone who expresses such recommendations is possibly overlooking an important issue. Dysfunctional behavior in the disclosed cases (and many other undisclosed cases) is not a consequence of the market economy as such. It is the result of faults in its regulatory framework, which were or are often caused by state interventions themselves.

The example of the much-maligned bankers or investment banks is a good illustration of this. Financial investors who act in their own self-interest will weigh risks carefully if they must bear all the consequences of their risk exposure themselves. They will only enter into a particular risky project under these conditions if the anticipated advantages exceed the anticipated disadvantages. If, instead, investors only pocket the profits of their investment in the event of a profit, but do not have to cover losses themselves in the event of a loss, then their decision-making processes are impaired. They will even find attractive those projects in which the anticipated losses clearly exceed the anticipated profit. This was the situation banks and other financial institutions found themselves in before the financial crisis (and actually still do today). In their liability for losses they are limited to their often very small amount of equity capital. They thus have incentives to enter into bets in which the possible profit is great, but also the possible loss is even greater, such that the expected value of these bets shows a negative return.[9]

In a system of free competition, the other party would act carefully: they would not make such deals in which the investors do not pay their obligations in the event of a loss. So banks with too little equity capital could not enter into such problematic bets, and the casino behavior on the financial markets would not become a problem at all. There is a problem if the liable equity capital is small but the bank finds business partners for their risky investments nevertheless, because in the event of a claim it is not the bank but the community or the taxpayer that shoulders the business partners' losses.

How should we approach this problem? Should we prohibit markets from dealing in risky investments? Should a regulatory body monitor investment behavior? Should we require investors to behave in a socially acceptable way, so that they are always bound to measure their investments against a social economic perspective? Or would it help if we obliged them to fund charitable projects? Such suggestions seem to chime with the prevailing social climate. But restrictions on investment freedom might have considerable side effects and would have a long-lasting negative impact on the innovatory power of the economy. And who but the investors themselves could best decide which projects are good or bad? Monitoring entrepreneurs with regard to their social conscience and "corporate social responsibility" is also difficult. And a few charitable deeds cannot compensate for the negative consequences of seriously bad investments.

A kind of therapy that targets the root causes looks somewhat different: it reforms the financial system in such a way that investors in the example in question must themselves bear the full consequences of their investment behavior. A banker acting in their own self-interest, who accepts all the profits as well as all the losses from their investment, will limit themselves to projects that create added value. In their own self-interest they will forego questionable projects. It is thus important to correct the faults in the regulatory framework, for example the notion of "too big to fail" or "too many to fail" in the context of the financial markets. Considerably increasing the equity capital requirements and other policies concerning the financial markets may, for example, contribute to bankers including possible losses from their investments in their calculations. The aim must be a system in which self-interested decisions once again chime with the goals of general economic prosperity. This is not always easy. Nevertheless, this path seems more promising than the attempt to replace a focus on individual self-interest with the "inoculation" of moral behavior in society.

To summarize: it is not the market-economic system or the self-interested behavior of economic actors that should be the focus of a critique of the system. Rather, it is regulatory mistakes and political failures that lead to suboptimal activities. What we need is a system of regulation that establishes the regulatory framework for economic activity in such a way that the self-interest of every individual economic actor can deploy its beneficial effect for the whole of society.

Notes

1. Susanne Schmidt, *Markt ohne Moral: Das Versagen der internationalen Finanzelite* (Munich: Droemer Knaur, 2010).

2. Reinhard Marx, *Das Kapital: Ein Plädoyer für den Menschen* (Munich: Pattloch, 2010). For this authorial quotation, cf. https://www.amazon.de/Das-Kapital-Ein-Pl%C3%A4doyer-Menschen/dp/3426783606/ref=pd_sim_14_1?_encoding=UTF8&psc=1&refRID=ZPN6N9AR0JCYC3BNJDWD (accessed November 30, 2017).

3. http://www.imdb.com/title/tt0094291/quotes (accessed November 30, 2017).

4. https://en.wikipedia.org/wiki/Michael_Milken (accessed November 30, 2017).

5. James B. Stewart, *Den of Thieves* (New York: Touchstone, 1992), p. 261.

6. Adam Smith, *An Inquiry into the Nature and Causes of the Wealth of Nations* (1776), Book IV, Chapter 2.

7. Gérard Debreu, *Theory of Value: An Axiomatic Analysis of Economic Equilibrium* (New York: Wiley, 1959).

8. Milton Friedman, "The Social Responsibility of Business is to Increase its Profits" in *The New York Times Magazine* (September 13, 1970), http://umich.edu/~thecore/doc/Friedman.pdf (accessed November 30, 2017).

9. A general analysis of these incentives, and one that anticipated the financial crisis, can be found, for example, in Hans-Werner Sinn, "Kinked Utility and the Demand for Human Wealth and Liability Insurance" in *European Economic Review* vol. 17, issue 2 (1982), pp. 149–62.

CHAPTER 10

ENTREPRENEURIAL ACTIVITY AND THE COMMON GOOD—A PLEA

ROLAND BERGER

I have chosen a somewhat different perspective on the subject of the common good, namely that of the entrepreneur and the company manager. I would like to show the extent to which entrepreneurial activity can and should contribute to the common good, but also how entrepreneurs and managers should be guided by the idea of the common good and their optimal contribution to it. I believe that companies can best contribute to increasing the common good if they focus on their core tasks: creating value for the individual and the community.

I am convinced that in our market-based economic system rooted in the division of labor, companies fundamentally contribute most to the common good when they are fully committed to their business. As Adam Smith said: "Individual ambition serves the common good." His "invisible hand" was the mechanism that, through goods and services, created the maximum common good out of individual self-interest, that is, above all, the pursuit of profit by competing for the buyer's favor.

Companies provide society with innovative goods and services at the best possible prices and conditions most of all when they are successful. And they create increasingly productive and more people-friendly jobs that offer workers employment, qualifications, and income. Ultimately, they increase the assets of their investors by realizing profits and distributing them in part or in full. These are the three core tasks of a company in a society that is organized along market economy lines. This is how they can best contribute to the common good.

In the last few years an idea has emerged concerning the concept of so-called corporate social responsibility, which says that alongside their core business, companies should make more effort to promote the common good, for example financing social institutions, environmental projects, or cultural organizations. However, as a rule such promotions detract from the actual core business. They can burden the business with costs, and because they have nothing to do with the core business they can also lessen or even jeopardize a company's contribution to the common good.

This is particularly applicable in the case of companies where management and owners are separate. Managers are agents of the investors and must serve their interest in the optimum/maximum realization of profits by providing people with goods and services in the best possible way, and by creating and productively maintaining jobs to do this. The owners can then decide for themselves how much of their profit they consume or would like to spend on charitable ends such as culture, education, health, or help for people in need, and how much they want to invest in the entrepreneurial activities of the distributing company or in other companies in which they want to invest.

Of course, in the case of owner-managers, who devote their entire work and financial resources to the company that they own 100 percent, this separation does not apply. As owners, they are free to decide how the profits should be invested in the core business of the company they own, or in part for other, perhaps charitable ends.

This separation of resources for core business activities from other financial resources and contributions that are allocated to charity beyond these core activities is increasingly a concern of corporate governance and compliance regulations as well as tax law. Both increasingly oblige company managers to make expenditure only for purposes that, at least indirectly, provide demonstrable benefits for the company's core tasks. In tax terms, this obligation applies to the separation of expenses for the core task of a company from expenses for other purposes even in the case of the owner-manager.

In the end, it should be said, particularly with regard to a company's contribution to the common good: "The business of a businessman is his business." Special institutions in civil society and the state itself are much better at looking after a society's common good in a transparent way.

CHAPTER 11

THE *PUBLIC VALUE ATLAS*: MEASURING THE COMMON GOOD?

TIMO MEYNHARDT

I. TOWARDS A NEW APPROACH

In fall 2017, the third *Public Value Atlas Switzerland,* using 14,500 respondents, was published. In Germany, the next post-2015 Atlas is in preparation.[1] A similar study is also being planned for Austria.

In these *Atlases,* a representative population sample of people aged between 18 and 90 evaluate in each case between five and six of the largest and best-known organizations and companies in their country. On a scale of 1 (disagree) to 6 (agree), this determines to what extent an organization is seen to contribute to the common good in four dimensions: task fulfillment ("performs well in its core business"); quality of life ("contributes to the quality of life in country x); social cohesion ("contributes to the social cohesion in country x"); and morality ("behaves decently"). The respondents could only evaluate organizations if they had sufficient knowledge of them. This produces a classification comprising 100 to 120 institutions.

The extensive media response and companies' and organizations' intense interest in these studies indicate the increased need for focus and reassurance when it comes to the topic of the common good. Why is this?

On the one hand, the very concept is undergoing a renaissance in a world that is increasingly felt to be unsafe. For example, Pope Francis I often evokes the common good in his sermons. As he insisted most recently during his visit to Colombia in September 2017, the individual, their value, and respect for the common good must be at the heart of all political, social, and economic activity. In the papal encyclical "On Care for our Common Home," Francis uses the term no fewer than 28 times.

On the other hand, while the academic world debates (over and over again) whether businesses should be subject to the common good, business practice itself blazes a trail and develops new approaches. It is not a question of whether top management wants to take on board its own business's contribution to the common good. Today, no one can any longer escape this debate. Indeed, a company neglecting its contribution to the common good could, as a result of negative consequences in its economic performance (customers staying away, the company not being prioritized by employees), create a liability case for the management.

The economic giants themselves demonstrate how they now incorporate the message of the common good in their work. For example, it is Google's stated aim, "to organize the world's information and make it universally accessible and useful." McDonald's regards itself as a *"Weltbürger mit Verantwortung"* [world citizen with responsibility], and Bayer stands for "Science for a Better Life." Today, there is hardly any major business that would not want to be seen as partnering society in the management of global challenges. Not least, the digital world's disruptive business models contain value propositions that aim directly to improve living conditions on our planet. We should constantly examine whether word and deed are consistent with each other. Many accuse global businesses of cynicism, but why should we not give them the opportunity to prove themselves?

This is where the idea of the *Public Value Atlas* comes in. If we look at the current Swiss findings, we can see that much has changed with regard to the common good in Switzerland since the last survey in 2015, and also the extent to which this has happened. Today, Swiss citizens are much more concerned that too little attention is being paid to the common good in Switzerland: 73 percent are of this opinion, a rise of 12 percent. But alongside this concern there is a simultaneous growth in the appreciation of what already exists: most organizations and businesses increased their positive rating. This may be because of the overall increase in insecurity due to global events by comparison with 2015, which led to circumstances in Switzerland being regarded less critically than hitherto. It should also be noted, however, that in all previous studies civil society institutions, whether public or semi-state-owned, or even cooperatives, were held in the highest esteem, while commercial enterprises attained medium to lower ratings.

But what actually is the *Public Value Atlas?* Who benefits from it? First of all, it is not just another opinion poll among many others that organizations commission and use for their own ends. Addressing the topic of the common good means something more and something different. There are three interconnected functions linked to the *Atlas*.[2]

1. PLACING THE COMMON GOOD ON THE AGENDA IN A NEW AND DIFFERENT WAY

Since Aristotle's discussion of the common good in the *polis*, the concept has been on the agenda and has concerned anyone who engages with the way large social groups function. Thus the history of the concept is long, ambiguous—and forward-facing. However, one should not oversimplify it and ultimately reduce the common good to one defined thing, in the sense of "…is nothing other than…." Such a fixed definition would guarantee but a short half-life. We need only think of the attempts by economists, politicians, or even lawyers to co-opt it.

An approach that is more likely to succeed, albeit more laborious, is to understand the common good in Immanuel Kant's sense of a regulatory idea, that is, one of the intellectual concepts that regulate human coexistence. As such it is certainly not abstract, but rather develops its power through the emotions linked to it. This means that it is dependent on the people who can develop and change it. In principle, it is first and foremost a mechanism of large groups without which sociality is not possible.

The common good is a necessary fiction—providing a focus, as it were, on the greater good, which only then takes shape, and which as a result has a regulatory effect. To evoke an image, the idea of the common good is like the function of a polestar that can never be reached but can always indicate a direction. This functional meaning is particularly relevant when everything all around is changing, nothing seems constant, and many things are placed in doubt. At precisely this moment, we should look for a deeper reason why, in times of great uncertainty but also of big opportunities, the focus on the common good reveals its motivating and organizing power. We might even say that if complexity is the challenge, the common good is the answer.

A society is unable to function if its members do not develop an idea of the common good that supports the community. This is well known to all in a secular community who (have to) deal with the common good, ultimately through complex trade-offs. There are clearly various terms for the notion of the common good, terms that emphasize individual aspects: community spirit, social harmony, cultural identity, etc. It is important to see that in each case these can only be approximations and temporary solutions, as regulatory ideas in particular cannot be defined in their totality.

As a result, the substance of the common good is constantly rebooted and appropriated in different ways depending on ideological and political attitudes. Occasionally, perception of the common good must be repaired and refocused in order to achieve a minimum consensus in society. In this situation, the question of what is in the "public interest" and what in the "interest of the country" arises more and more frequently.

The *Public Value Atlas* is new and different in two respects: first, it draws upon a frame of reference borrowed from the scientifically based psychology of needs. In this, the collective level of the common good is confronted with and related to the *conditio humana*. The elusive common good is linked to individual experience and translated from the theoretical sphere into the realm of everyday life. This gives the common good a basis that is empirically verifiable as opposed to soap-box speeches, metaphysical exercises, and abstract mind games. More fulfillment of societal needs = more common good—this is the simple formula. Anyone wanting to invoke other frames of reference can of course do so.

Our approach is based on a holistic view of humanity, open to different forms of development and variations of basic needs. By linking the individual with the collective via the concept of the common good, we can address the relationship between a (supposedly) self-creating and powerful subject and an increasingly unmanageable and alienating society, a relationship that has become very complicated in the modern world.

A second, important idea forms the backbone of the *Public Value Atlas*. In the spirit of Peter Drucker, the influential pioneer of modern management, our organizations and their actions are ascribed a role that is particularly relevant to the common good. Here we are focusing not primarily on the common good as enshrined in legal texts, in religious writings, or in abstract principles of state, but rather the common good that is produced by small and large organizations every day in the course of their ordinary lives. It is our institutions—in other words, businesses, public administration, and NGOs in particular—that characterize, shape, and even change our sense of the common good.

From this perspective, the concept of value creation that is common in business administration also gains an extended and partly new meaning. Organizations not only make a contribution to the common good: we might put it even more strongly and pointedly and say that they are actively *creating* society. Through organizational experiences as a customer, employee, or citizen, we have social experiences that affect the structures of our needs and thereby form a context for personal development. The common good thus becomes a basic condition of human self-development and its servant. The common good is therefore not an end in itself. The individual can use the common good as a social resource, which they can at best rely upon, and from which they can draw strength and confidence.

One example of the special role played by businesses and their entrepreneurial activity is without question in digitalization. After all, the current surge in scientific and technological progress in the form of digitalization promises a much greater convergence of people and technology, thus changing the framework of the individual's personal development and social experience. As always in periods of technological euphoria, people say that this time it will be totally different and new heights of quality will really be achieved. In fact, there is much to indicate that the personal and global experience of all of us can be mediated or even completely re-imagined by means of technological devices more than ever before.

If we see the common good as a condition of the individual's possibility of a successful life, digitalization promises a massive transformation of the "conditions" of the common good. If our ways of interacting temporally, socially, and spatially with other people, with institutions, and also with the material world, and not least with ourselves change under the influence of technology, this leads to a massive transformation in living conditions. Previous experiences of self-efficacy, group membership, and freedom could at least be supplemented by the digital transformation, and in some cases even replaced or destroyed. In this sense, the digital transformation is a driver of new forms of the common good and thus a new breeding ground for the experience of subjectivity and successful interaction with one's social environment.

2. MEASURING WHAT CAN REASONABLY BE MEASURED

Creating an *Atlas* means measuring something and, as a result, characterizing an internal context. But is it not arrogant to speak about "measurement" in this case? Probably not, if we accept that the survey approach is based on transparent quality standards and is verifiable. Drawing on many individual opinions and bringing them together as an average value becomes the attempt to find a common denominator to describe socially shared values. What is important here is traceability and plausibility, not a claim to accuracy that is associated with a scientific ideal but unachievable.

In the first place, it is a survey about individual organizations created using the tools of social scientific methodology, or more precisely it is about the images of such organizations we have in our heads and actively associate with them at the moment the questionnaire is completed. These images are never simple representations of a reality that we merely have to identify. No—they are the result of diverse external influences, but also internal states. For example, when we evaluate others (in this instance actual organizations), we are of course always saying something about ourselves. This is not surprising when people themselves are the measuring instrument. What else could serve as a thermometer for the condition of a society? This addresses a quite fundamental issue in any research into the common good. At least since the pioneering observations of philosopher Immanuel Kant, we have been aware of the impossibility of perceiving our environment in a way that is independent of the observer.

In everyday life, however, we try to suppress this very insight (later named the uncertainty principle), and we try to avoid the accompanying epistemological uncertainty.

The *Public Value Atlas* affects our self-image in two ways: first, as a participant in the questionnaire, it is about my own understanding of the organizations that surround me or influence me. Thus I am asked for value judgments and I have to come clean about what individual organizations are worth to me. The *Atlas* is designed in such a way that everyone can set their own weighting and thus create their individual definition of the common good. It is not about the passive expression of opinions, but about active participation in the debate.

Of course, it is very easy to express an opinion. But seeing such a questionnaire as a simple ticking of boxes against slogans would fall short of the mark and not take people seriously. This would be snobbish and ultimately anti-democratic. It is not about fluctuating opinions, but about consolidated experience, getting to the heart (or in this case the tick-box) of attitudes and values.

Whether we like it or not, we are talking about a mental reality that is neither true nor false, but just real. But beware: the *Public Value Atlas* is not a simple representation of this. Rather, placing a tick against statements creates this reality in the first place. To some extent this reality is induced and implemented by the survey process itself. Or, more precisely, commonly referring to the common good as a fictional "as-if" produces a so-called collective systemic parameter, which in turn creates a focus.

We can—indeed must—argue at length about how we can reasonably increase the accuracy of these common references. There is at least no social scientifically viable option that obviates the aggregation of individual opinions as the best possible approach to collective phenomena. In any event, the *Atlas* is an inter-subjectively generated and thus social representation of the state of consciousness of a carefully selected subset of the population.

All in all, it is about a collective self-understanding, that is, an expression of the collective soul, the common emotional ecology. How can we be satisfied with ourselves if the environment is not right? But how strongly do I feel obliged to assume responsibility for taking my fate into my own hands? To this extent, "good" organizations not only contribute to our individual life satisfaction, they also stimulate motivation and energy for life. Humans are indeed social beings, who can define themselves as individuals only when face to face[3] with others. Without a "you" or a "we," an "I" is inconceivable. Seen in this way, the *Public Value Atlas* is a tool or a visual aid to articulate mutual dependencies using social science-based methodology.

3. FROM ITEM OF VOCABULARY VIA LANGUAGE TO DIALOGUE

The common good is one of those concepts that have been invoked in the cultural history of humanity again and again as a call to arms or a wake-up call, in order to appeal to the "whole." It is a perfect way of mobilizing political energies and/or disguising individual interests. Equally, one can also try to suspend use of the concept completely. It is important to remember the image of society conveyed by the stakeholder approach in the study of business management. In this, all relationships between businesses and their environment are reduced to individual relationships, in which the actors each have control over their own demands. The seemingly intractable greater good is reduced to concrete relationships and thus disappears from view.

And yet, good concepts can withstand even this over the course of time and renew themselves from within. The common good seems to be just such a self-righting vessel, which from time to time is not only in danger of appropriation, but also suffers from a lack of specificity. This is especially true when it degenerates into an empty formula or is downgraded to a mere item of vocabulary.

The writer Martin Walser articulates the difference between "vocabulary" and "language" with razor sharpness: for him language "always becomes vocabulary when it is intended positively ... Language can be experienced. Vocabulary is understandable ... Language does not have to be correct. Vocabulary is correct."[4] Similarly, the *Public Value Atlas* does not have to be "correct," but it should make our social reality more accessible to experience. The ever-present problem of measuring in each survey is thus relativized to a certain extent, if we place more emphasis on the *Public Value Atlas*'s incentive to articulate and reflect on our own social experience. For, to echo Immanuel Kant, what are intuitions without concepts, and concepts without intuitions?

Alienation begins where the conversation ends, where it is reduced to the exchange of items of vocabulary, or is thought and felt in the form of mutual prejudices and condemnations. Being in conversation with each other also means creating common experiences.

And this is the core of the whole: the common good can only be experienced, not defined.

To this extent, the *Public Value Atlas* is also a resonating space, a unique quasi-object,[5] which provides reference points for the debate. The *Public Value Atlas* creates a public realm for the common good.

It is clear: initially, we see just bare numerical values, which reveal their meaning only through interpretation and thereby bring to light or bring to life a "truth." It would be wrong to search immediately for reasons and causes. We will simply not find them if we do not first of all (and this is by no means meant therapeutically) pay attention to our inner voice and find out for ourselves what is important to us about this topic.

Moreover, trying to uncover the common good empirically is a deeply democratic matter. Who else but the people should be able to pronounce on this? They are the sovereign body itself that has the legitimacy and the voice to speak about social conditions. Historically, no social system can survive without subjective acceptance. Anyone who underestimates the subjective question runs the risk of underestimating a very important dimension of social stability, as well as the capacity to innovate.

II. SUMMARY

The *Public Value Atlas* is a mirror that society holds up to its organizations. Whether they recognize themselves in the image or not is one issue. Another issue concerns society itself, which projects its attitudes onto the *Atlas*. The *Public Value Atlas* is also an expression of a collective emotional ecology, in which an internal system or even cultural self-knowledge is unfolded. It condenses public opinion and raises it to the level of a published opinion. This is not a metaphysical exercise, but rather a practical, collective self-reflection as the basis for a debate and discussion focused on the reality of life.

This is where the idea of seeing the common good as a condition of the possibility of a successful life comes into play—or, more succinctly, "no freedom without the common good." The common good becomes the basic condition of human self-development.

We can now answer the question, "*cui bono?*": in the best case, the *Public Value Atlas* benefits all of us, each individual in his or her own position, and those organizations who want to communicate their role and impact in society and build new bridges.

In the future, it will be important to improve accuracy of measurement and find alternative forms of data collection. However, alongside this ongoing challenge, it is most important to explore the opportunities and limits of the debate stimulated by the *Public Value Atlas*. This includes, for example, the fusion of the material and intellectual foundations that lead to corresponding value judgments in the population.

One thing seems certain: it is the disruptive dynamics of current developments in the economy and society that will continue to drive the search for the common good and the compatibility of business and political activity with the common good. In this context, the *Public Value Atlas* can make an empirically based contribution to self-assurance. This is particularly important in a culture of debate where opinion, evaluation, and belief are characterized by polarization and driven by dynamic changes.

This approach should be particularly interesting for those who want to shape their environment, and in so doing recognize how they themselves (whether as a business or as an individual) can depend on and influence the common good in their development.

Notes

1. See http://www.gemeinwohl.ch and http://www.gemeinwohlatlas.de.

2. This essay draws in part on Timo Meynhardt and Peter Gomez's contribution, "Was dient der Allgemeinheit? Und wer?" in *Wirtschaftswoche* (October 30, 2015) and on T. Meynhardt, "Ohne Gemeinwohl keine Freiheit: zur Psychologie des Gemeinwohls" in *Freiheit und Gemeinwohl*, ed. by Hans-Jürgen Papier and Timo Meynhardt (Berlin: Tempus Corporate, 2016), pp. 173–92.

3. Emmanuel Levinas, *Totality and Infinity: An Essay on Exteriority* (Dordrecht: Kluwer Academic Publishers, 1991).

4. Martin Walser, *Die Verwaltung des Nichts. Aufsätze* (Berlin: Reinbek, 2004), pp. 72, 89.

5. Bruno Latour, *We Have Never Been Modern*, trans. Catherine Porter (Cambridge MA: Harvard University Press, 1993).

CHAPTER 12

THE FUTURE OF EMPLOYMENT

CARL BENEDIKT FREY

Convoco interviewed Dr Carl Benedikt Frey, one of the most widely cited scholars in the field of workforce automation, about AI, industrial renewal, and the common good.

Together with machine-learning researcher Michael Osborne, he published a widely recognized study about the loss of jobs through automation.[1] By examining 702 jobs in the US, the study shows how susceptible jobs are to computerization. According to their assessment, 47 percent of total US employment is in the high-risk category, i.e. they are jobs that could be automated relatively soon, perhaps over the next decade or two. This would mean a dramatic change in our society.

Carl Benedikt Frey is Oxford Martin Citi Fellow and co-directs the Oxford Martin Programme on Technology and Employment, a leading program on the future of work, which researches the transition of industrial nations to digital economies.

Convoco: What do you think of the following statement by the inventor of HTML and founder of the World Wide Web, Tim Berners Lee: "It is difficult to argue against the thought that artificial intelligence will in the future be smarter than human intelligence and could thus take over the world."

Carl Benedikt Frey: Artificial intelligence is already outperforming humans in a variety of tasks, such as chess, Jeopardy!, and more recently even Go. But general artificial intelligence is a different matter. No algorithm outperforms humans in every single task. We still hold the comparative advantage in complex social interactions and creative tasks, for example. It is of course possible that the comparative advantage of humans will vanish in those domains as well, but for the time being that future seems distant.

C: What made you start your research on the link between AI, computerization, and the future of employment?

CBF: Our understanding of the potential social and economic consequences of AI has not been keeping pace with how fast the technology has been developing. Our models no longer reflect technological and economic reality as algorithms are getting better at a variety of tasks, such as driving a car, performing medical diagnostics, and translation work. What got me and my engineering sciences colleagues in Oxford started on this topic was trying to understand what recent technological advances in artificial intelligence and mobile robotics are likely to mean for the workforce in the future.

C: Do you think that AI and computerization are beneficial to the idea of the common good?

CBF: On average, automation has always benefited society, but sometimes at the expense of large parts of the workforce whose jobs have disappeared. It is up to society to make computerization a common good by making sure that its benefits are widely shared. It is not a common good *per se*.

C: Is there a big divergence in how and when computerization hits the different continents and differently developed worlds? Let us say that computerization hits the jobs of low- and high-skilled workers in Europe and Asia first, is there a chance people might wish to emigrate to Africa and South America, reversing current migration trends, in order to find jobs?

CBF: Despite the promise of the digital economy to make geography redundant, it has done exactly the opposite. Since the computer revolution of the 1980s, new jobs have increasingly clustered in places with a highly skilled workforce, such as London, Stockholm, and Munich, while places that have specialized in low-skilled jobs are likely to see a large share of their labor force being automated away. It used to be an advantage to have an abundance of cheap labor to be able to produce at lower cost. With advances in automation, that advantage is gradually disappearing. This is likely to exacerbate current trends in migration from low- to high-income countries. The problem is likely to be particularly great in Africa where the population is growing fast, but manufacturing industry is creating very few jobs. The current migration crisis is likely to be minor compared to the forthcoming one, as a large part of Africa's population will search for jobs elsewhere.

C: Is creativity and lateral thinking a domain that will remain firmly in the hands of human intelligence, or will it also be taken over by artificial intelligence?

CBF: At least for now, creativity seems to remain firmly in the hands of humans. Over the much longer term this is obviously an open question.

C: Can you give us a positive outlook on the impact of computerization?

CBF: Over the very long term, automation has always been an engine of comfort and prosperity: during Britain's Industrial Revolution, the benefits of automation initially went to the owners of capital: it took six decades for workers to see its benefits, but then finally, between 1840 and 1900, real wages grew by 123 percent. It is possible that we are seeing history repeating itself. Indeed, the economic trajectories of the computer revolution so far closely resemble those of the Industrial Revolution. But if many workers lose out to automation in the short term, they are likely to take a stand against it. Our research shows that the recent rise of populism is in part driven by workers who have lost out to automation.

We are only at the early beginnings of the automation challenge: in advanced economies, roughly half of all jobs are at risk of automation in the near future as a result of recent developments in artificial intelligence. In the same way that the Industrial Revolution transformed manufacturing, a "de-industrial revolution" is now under way that is promising to revolutionize services in similar fashion. As more and more jobs become exposed to automation, further political rebellion is likely, unless we make sure that the benefits of automation become more widely shared.

C: Working is an important element of identity. If we lose this, what is going to replace it? Are we at a turning point in history?

CBF: To be sure, our jobs are an important part of our identity. But clearly, social norms have changed in the past and could do so also in the future. If our main concern becomes how to occupy our leisure time, people will have to form their identities around things other than their jobs. And some already do. But it would without doubt be a turning point in history and not an easy transition.

C: If you had to make a prediction, what would you say working life will look like in ten years' time?

CBF: Over the past century, automation has relieved us from the most physically demanding, dangerous, and boringly repetitive jobs. As automation progresses in the near future, humans will still hold the comparative advantage in creativity and social intelligence. In other words, we will have to re-allocate our labor to the things we enjoy the most. I suspect that for workers that have the relevant skills working life will be much more interesting and enjoyable in ten years' time. My worry is that many workers who do not have such skills will be left behind in the transition.

C: What is your biggest worry for the future of mankind? Do you fear that humans will make themselves redundant?

CBF: The only thing we know about the future is that we are pretty bad at predicting it. It has always been a known unknown. Since the early days of the Industrial Revolution, people have worried that humans will automate themselves into obsolescence. Today, a still frequent belief is that the human worker will go down the route of the horse, whose role in artillery, transportation, and agriculture was gradually displaced, and whose use by humans has now been reduced to mainly ceremonial purposes and sporting events. The reason that the human worker did not experience the same fate as the horse is our insatiable demand for services, which we lack the technological capabilities to automate. Of course, it is entirely possible that technology at some point might be able to fulfill all of our demands. In such an event, our main concern will be how to distribute the gains from technology and how to occupy our leisure time. For now, such a future seems remote.

Note

1. C.B. Frey and M.A. Osborne, "The Future of Employment: How Susceptible are Jobs to Computerisation?" in *Technological Forecasting and Social Change* vol. 114, (2017), pp. 254–280. https://doi.org/10.1016/j.techfore.2016.08.019 (accessed November 21, 2017).

CHAPTER 13

WHAT IS THE IMPACT OF DIGITALIZATION ON THE LABOR MARKET?

JÖRG ROCHOLL

Innovation and technological progress are essential conditions for sustainable economic prosperity. This statement has almost acquired the character of a truism, as it is a mantra of both companies and governments to attach great importance to boosting innovation—and they encounter no serious opposition to this. On the contrary, they are more likely to be criticized for not doing enough to promote and support new developments, especially in times of extensive technological change affecting almost all sectors of society.

In this context, it is often overlooked that innovation and technological progress do not always offer benefits for every individual or even for larger groups. What is good on average does not necessarily apply to a cross-section of society. In the last century, Josef Schumpeter coined the concept of "creative destruction," in which companies, in their efforts to succeed competitively through innovation, create new structures and at the same time destroy old ones. In the face of this destruction of existing structures, innovation and technological progress are often accompanied by skepticism and fear, in particular by workers in traditional industries who fear for the survival of their jobs. Particularly prominent examples are the 19th-century Luddites in the textile industry, who destroyed mechanized looms as they were worried about their jobs, or the introduction of the assembly line at the beginning of the 20th century, which provoked major debates about the future of work. A similarly profound impact is expected today as a result of developments in the worlds of digitalization and artificial intelligence—an impact which has to some extent already happened. Thus it becomes all the more important to ask what challenges these developments will present with regard to the labor market, and how we should respond to them.

I. POLANYI'S PARADOX AND THE COMPLEMENTARY NATURES OF WORK AND TECHNOLOGY

Taking the longer view, we can see that, despite all the concerns, innovation and technological progress have not led to a sustained rise in unemployment thus far. On the contrary, both the total number of those in employment and economic prosperity have risen massively over the last century. Today's workers have at their disposal a purchasing power that would have been inconceivable to their ancestors a hundred years ago, not to mention the innumerable qualitative improvements that technological and economic achievements have brought with them.

These developments stand in remarkable contrast to generally accepted expectations and beliefs, according to which jobs would necessarily become superfluous as a result of automation, and as a result unemployment would have to rise in the long run. So if we wonder why the demand for work is not declining while automation is simultaneously increasing, then two considerations are of particular significance. First, we must take account of the substantial value of implicit knowledge, which can be described as follows in the context of Polanyi's Paradox:[1] "We know more than we can tell."[2] Second, it is not the case that work and technology can consistently substitute for one another. Rather, they are often complementary, and more (or better) technology can even lead to work acquiring a higher value. The economist David Autor explains:

> When we break an egg over the edge of a mixing bowl, identify a distinct species of birds based only on a fleeting glimpse, write a persuasive paragraph, or develop a hypothesis to explain a poorly understood phenomenon, we are engaging in tasks that we only tacitly understand how to perform. Following Polanyi's observation, the tasks that have proved most vexing to automate are those demanding flexibility, judgment and common sense—skills that we understand only tacitly. [...] The fact that a task cannot be computerized does not imply that computerization has no effect on that task. On the contrary: tasks that cannot be substituted by computerization are generally complemented by it. This point is as fundamental as it is overlooked. Most work processes draw upon a multifaceted set of inputs: labor and capital; brains and brawn; creativity and rote repetition; technical mastery and intuitive judgment; perspiration and inspiration; adherence to rules and judicious application of discretion. Typically, these inputs each play essential roles; that is, improvements in one do not obviate the need for the other. If so, productivity improvements in one set of tasks almost necessarily increase the economic value of the remaining tasks.[3]

Two points in Autor's argument deserve particular attention. First, not all human activities can be automated—so far at least. Those tasks in particular that demand flexibility and judgment elude simple description by algorithms and therefore their translation into automated processes. Complex and intricate problems thus require the use of human judgment and creativity. Second, the automation of one input factor in a work process can raise the economic value of the other input factors in the same process. One concrete example to illustrate this is the assembly line production of cars. In the last century, the introduction of this kind of production may have led to concern that a smaller labor force would be needed to build a single car, and that unemployment would have to rise as a result. However, this overlooked the fact that the gains in production efficiency first and foremost created the opportunity of making a mass-market product out of a commodity that was once unaffordable for most workers, and as a result lots of new employment opportunities arose that were not automatable to the same extent. Alongside suppliers, we might think of the sectors of design and development, sales, or finance.

II. THE PARTICULAR CHALLENGES OF DIGITALIZATION AND ARTIFICIAL INTELLIGENCE

The central question in the current debate about economic policy can best be summarized as follows: will it be different *this* time? Can digitalization and AI succeed in resolving Polanyi's Paradox by automating even those processes that were considered non-automatable, and that were thus not suitable for simple programming? Even in 1961 an article in *Time* magazine was talking about "The Automation Jobless" and stated:

> Throughout industry, the trend has been to bigger production with a smaller work force ... Many of the losses in factory jobs have been countered by an increase in the service industries or in office jobs. But automation is beginning to move in and eliminate office jobs too ... In the past, new industries hired far more people than those they put out of business. But this is not true of many of today's new industries ... Today's new industries have comparatively few jobs for the unskilled or semiskilled, just the class of workers whose jobs are being eliminated by automation.[4]

Even then, concern was being articulated that administrative jobs too might fall victim to automation. While this concern has thus far proved to be widely unfounded, this is not sufficient proof that this will remain the case in the future. Since then, the capabilities of computers, which have grown considerably since the *Time* article, can even replace skilled professions—for example jobs such as accounting, auditing, or invoicing. In this, particular significance is attributed to so-called machine learning, a particular application of AI, which enables machines to learn autonomously, and thus to understand processes that have so far eluded explicit coding, in the sense of Polanyi's Paradox. David H. Autor describes machine learning thus:

> The simple idea of machine learning is applying statistics and inductive reasoning to supply best-guess answers in cases where formal procedural rules are unknown. Where engineers are unable to program a machine to "simulate" a nonroutine task by following a scripted procedure, they may nevertheless be able to program a machine to master the task autonomously by studying successful examples of the task being carried out by others. Thus, through a process of exposure, training, and reinforcement, machine learning algorithms may potentially infer how to accomplish tasks that have proved dauntingly challenging to codify with explicit procedures.

Similarly, in 2016 a publication which became known as the *Oxford Report* argued:

> Our work also suggests the scope of technology change is increasing. The big data revolution and improvements in machine learning algorithms means that more occupations can be replaced by technology, including tasks once thought quintessentially human such as navigating a car or deciphering handwriting.[6]

The crucial question is thus whether AI will reverse the long-term tendency of automation not to entail a loss of jobs. Assessments concerning this question vary enormously, without being able to reach a consensus thus far. Ben Y. Zhao of the University of Chicago takes a rather pessimistic view:

> I think AI will kill jobs, and over time, AI might kill most "jobs" as we know them. I think that people are somewhat complacent in regard to the economic impact of AI, and will likely be ill-prepared for the changes we have to adapt to in the not-so-distant future [...] But I would argue that AI is fundamentally different from machinery or most of the other analogies commonly made when answering this question, because AI is growing and is unlikely to stop growing. It's growing in breadth (of applications and industries), in geographic and economic scope, and in power (its capacity to address increasingly complex tasks). A more fitting analogy would be machinery in an automobile plant that not only made the parts one

day, but then learned how to assemble them the week after, and then how to design cars a year later. [...] I am far from original in this opinion.[7]

Stephen Hawking goes further and fears that the full development of AI might mean the end of humankind.[8]

By contrast, Autor takes a more sanguine view:

The long-term potential of machine learning for circumventing Polanyi's Paradox is a subject of active debate among computer scientists. Some researchers expect that as computing power rises and training databases grow, the brute force machine learning approach will approach or exceed human capabilities. Others suspect that machine learning will only ever "get it right" on average while missing many of the most important and informative exceptions [...] In 1900, for example, 41 percent of the United States workforce was employed in agriculture. By 2000, that share had fallen to 2 percent [...] It is unlikely, however, that farmers at the turn of the 20th century could foresee that 100 years later, healthcare, finance, information technology, consumer electronics, hospitality, leisure and entertainment would employ far more workers than agriculture.[9]

If there is no consensus on the question of the development of the aggregated demand for labor, there are at least three developments that distinguish today's technological change from earlier developments—on this subject see the *Oxford Report*. First, the speed of technological change has increased, and is described as much faster and more disruptive than earlier developments. Second, it is increasing in scale. This can be seen, for example, if we look at how many areas of the economy and society are currently debating the effects of digitalization—not least in universities. Third, many digital business models follow the principle of "winner takes all." This leads to new questions about the distribution of economic prosperity.

III. APPROACHES TO A POSSIBLE SOLUTION

In summarizing these arguments it is indisputable that the effects of new technologies can be substantial, even if their specific characteristics are not clear at the moment. This raises the question of how opportunities can best be used and possible negative consequences softened.

One suggested solution that is often discussed is the creation of an unconditional basic income, in which every citizen of a country receives an income in return for no work. This is intended to allow the citizen to maintain a certain minimum standard of living even without employment. This suggestion has been articulated in various countries, for example in the US and Germany, interestingly even by leading industrialists in particular. Alongside the fundamental question of affordability, depending on the targeted level of income, several serious criticisms arise in this context. First, an unconditional basic income can reduce the incentives for workers to engage with the labor market, with a corresponding reduction in labor supply and the risk of creating parallel societies of workers and non-workers. Second, work represents much more than the generation of income; to a considerable extent it has an impact on the individual's social engagement and the coherence of societies. Thus an unconditional basic income is an inadequate substitute for work. Third, if it is paid out randomly to all citizens of a country, the knock-on effects would be enormous. Fourth, it has immediate effects on the question of open state borders, as an unconditional basic income can lead to adverse selection in the case of migration.

A more sensible alternative is reform of the education system, both in vocational training and further education. Some suggestions on how to do this can be outlined: on the one hand, coding should become an obligatory component of curricula in schools and universities, as the fourth basic skill alongside reading, writing, and arithmetic. In addition, the basic understanding of information technologies should occupy a much larger position in vocational training and further education. On the other hand, opportunities should be created for employees to have sabbaticals or so-called "pit stops" throughout their careers in order to undertake qualifications and further education. Workers today can look forward to an ever-lengthening lifespan, which because of demographic imbalances should also lead to an increase in working life. At the same time, the speed of technological change has a tendency to increase, with the result that workers will encounter more and more new developments that they did not learn about during their early education.

Digitalization and AI present the economy, politics, and society with new challenges. Today their effects are not yet known in every detail and are somewhat contested. It is important that in the case of all these challenges the available opportunities are used and made as accessible as possible. The common good will not benefit if people who are not thought capable of working with new technologies are encouraged to do nothing as a result of an unconditional basic income. Extensive efforts to improve educational opportunities will be more important for the common good in the long term, and will enable participation in economic progress and social exchange.

A central challenge in these developments will always be that it is not totally clear today which professions and economic sectors will be most seriously affected by this change. The market will play an important role as a testing ground in this process. In the long run, some of the innovations that seem very promising today may disappear without trace, while others that are less well known today might lead to massive disruptions in just a short period of time. The frank admission of this lack of knowledge is an essential condition for promoting and not impeding the important role of the market in this process.

Notes

1. David H. Autor, "Polanyi's Paradox and the Shape of Employment Growth" in *Reevaluating Labor Market Dynamics* (Federal Reserve Bank of St. Louis: Economic Policy Proceedings, 2015), pp. 129–77.

2. Cf. Michael Polanyi, *The Tacit Dimension* (London: Routledge, 1966).

3. David H. Autor, "Why are There Still so Many Jobs? The History and Future of Workplace Automation" in *Journal of Economic Perspectives*, vol. 29 (3) (2015), pp. 3–20.

4. "The Automation Jobless" in *Time* magazine (February 24, 1961).

5. Autor, "Polanyi's Paradox," op. cit., p. 159.

6. Cf. Carl Benedikt Frey and Michael Osborne, *Technology at Work. The Future of Innovation and Employment* (Oxford: Citi GPS: Global Perspectives & Solutions, 2015).

7. Ben Y. Zhao, "Will AI Kill Jobs?", https://www.quora.com/Will-AI-kill-jobs (accessed January 3, 2018).

8. Rory Cellan-Jones, "Stephen Hawking Warns Artificial Intelligence Could End Mankind" (December 2, 2014), http://www.bbc.com/news/technology-30290540 (accessed January 3, 2018).

9. Autor, "Why are There Still so Many Jobs?", op. cit., p. 26.

CHAPTER 14

THE COMMON GOOD: A LOOK AHEAD

CLEMENS FUEST

I. THE COMMON GOOD: WHAT IS IT AND WHAT HAS IT GOT TO DO WITH THE ACTIVITIES OF THE STATE?

What is the future of the common good? In order to determine this, we must have a clear idea of what the common good means today—an issue that can be argued over for a long time. When thinking about the common good, it is helpful, in my opinion, to start with the economic model illustrated by Robinson Crusoe. Let us imagine a society that comprises one person, living like Robinson Crusoe on an island. Economic activity plays a central role here. For example, Robinson decides to plant crops. This means he can invest in and rely on the resources the island puts at his disposal. However, there is no common good on this island, as Robinson Crusoe is alone and the common good is concerned with the coexistence of people and cooperation or conflict among them.

The topic of the common good becomes relevant when Friday appears on the scene. In a society consisting of two people, the question immediately arises of who decides what the common good is. Usually, economists assume that every responsible individual knows best what they want. So, for example, voluntary exchange is seen as a process that increases the common good. Exchange, especially in conjunction with the division of labor, enables considerable gains in prosperity, and the realization of such gains in prosperity is an important form of the common good.

The increase in the common good through the exchange of private goods at markets, as we know them, is characterized by the fact that under normal circumstances exchange only takes place when all participants agree. To this extent it is clear that everyone is in a better position, and as a result the common good increases. Nevertheless, the functioning of markets is not without preconditions. For example, it requires secure property rights. In modern societies, the state has the task of protecting property. There exist goods that are important for the common good, but which are not available or in demand in private markets, or only in a very inadequate way. Examples are public goods such as domestic security and national defense. Collective decisions are required to make these goods available. The financing of these goods must be as a result of compulsory levies. In the case of collective decisions, it is not guaranteed that the position of all those involved will be improved as a result of them.

Who defines what the common good is in a society? In autocratic societies, a king, a dictator, a single political party, or a religious leader claims the definition of what the common good is. In democratic and pluralistic constitutional states that is not possible. Here we should accept that citizens have very different notions of what the common good is. So the challenge lies in the fact that collective action to increase the common good needs joint decisions on how to deal with it. In order to translate individual ideas about the common good into such a decision, the democratic constitutional state uses decision-making processes. In a democracy, the most important decision-making process is majority voting. Does that mean we are voting on what is the common good?

The following quotation is attributed to Willy Brandt: "Democracy should not go so far that families vote on who the father is."

Without doubt, there are aspects of the common good that we do not want to leave to majority voting in a free constitutional state. For example, if parliament declares a certain group of people to be second-class citizens, this cannot be seen as a manifestation of the common good. This is why, in the democratic constitutional state, there are constitutional rules that limit majority decisions. However, these too are rules that came about at some point through voting. The constitutional legislator makes fundamental decisions about what the common good should be. In a free society, the goal of constitutional rules is to give the individual's development as much space as possible and to restrict freedoms only so far as is required because of conflicts between individuals or to guarantee the provision of public goods.

A sensible balance between decisions made as a result of majority voting and the restrictions on such decisions through constitutional rules and opt-in systems, for example through the establishment of a second chamber, should limit any abuse of power.

Among these "checks and balances" in the democratic constitutional state, there is also the binding of the state administration to current law, an independent judiciary, and not least a critical public sphere. Issues that will be put to the vote are discussed publicly. Participants in this public debate are citizens, political parties, experts, and also a variety of organizations, associations, interest groups, and so-called NGOs, which are also interest groups but frequently aim to define what the common good is in a particular area. As a rule, in the free, democratic constitutional state there is no consensus on what the common good is, but collective decisions are framed in such a way that a broad participation in decision-making processes takes place and individual rights are protected to some extent.

The common good can also be defined by people voting with their feet. When people abandon one kind of community and choose another one, they are signaling that for them the common good can be realized better in another community. This exit option has considerable significance: it protects minorities from exploitation and curbs the consequences of the abuse of power.

II. WHAT IS THE FUTURE OF THE COMMON GOOD?

We are living under the influence of various developments that bring with them opportunities as well as risks for the common good and the well-being of all of us. By this I do not mean challenges that are to a certain extent established, such as geopolitical tensions, migration, demographic change, global warming, or the digitalization and automation of the economy. My concern is how we manage these risks and, linked to this, our shared understanding of what the common good is and what we must do to serve the common good.

1. IS THERE A CONTRADICTION BETWEEN THE COMMON GOOD AND THE INDIVIDUAL GOOD?

An important issue for the future is surely the fundamental question of how we understand the common good. Many people understand the common good as the antithesis of the individual good, in the sense of public spirit versus self-will, altruism versus egotism. From this point of view, the common good seems to be about goodness and is of morally higher value. I consider this approach dangerous. In this situation, it is as if the individual good is standing in the way of the common good: it must be moved aside, managed, and diverted onto the right lines, thus ultimately leveraging the common good.

It seems to me much more meaningful to understand the common good as derived from the individual good. The common good simply does not exist as a good that is independent of the individual and of individual interests, for whoever decides what the common good is, does it from their own, individual perspective. As there are various notions about what the common good is, rules must be agreed for collective decisions. The result is not the common good, but rather a decision that has been legitimized by democratic processes—nothing more, but also nothing less.

2. DISENFRANCHISEMENT IN THE NANNY STATE

One much-discussed and constant concern of liberal thinkers such as Friedrich von Hayek has been that the continued proliferation of the welfare state has increasingly disenfranchised people. Since the 1970s, the welfare state has expanded, has on various occasions reached its limits, and has repeatedly had its limits set. Against the backdrop of today's techno-logical and economic changes such as digitalization and automation in the economy, there are increasing demands to introduce an unconditional basic income. Apart from practical problems such as affordability, it is in principle questionable whether it can serve the common good to give up on large sections of society, as it were, and no longer attempt to give them respon-sibility for earning their own living or integrate them into working life.

A more subtle variety of welfare state disenfran-chisement is the application of instruments such as "nudging." Normally, the state introduces rules, requirements, and prohibitions in order to achieve certain goals. Nudging is a softer kind of intervention. Nudges are defined as "soft ways of steering people in particular directions while preserving their freedom," potentially without them noticing it.

An app on a cellphone that tells us every morning how much exercise we did yesterday and how much unrefined sugar we consumed; a retirement plan to which we are automatically subscribed unless we opt out. These are more or less subtle attempts to control our behavior without our realizing it. Companies' marketing departments are paid to influence consumers in this way. We can take different views on this. The state's use of these instruments should not be regarded exclusively in negative terms, but when government agencies use them this should certainly be done under conditions of transparency.

III. THE INCREASING SEPARATION OF RESPONSIBILITY AND LIABILITY IN EUROPE

Over the course of the development of the European Monetary Union, a trend emerged towards joint liability for debts incurred by states and banks in Europe, in particular through the OMT (Outright Monetary Transactions) program of the European Central Bank and the various monetary policy programs through which sovereign debt was acquired. If this trend continues, we can look forward to a further destabilization of Europe's currency and public finances. Therefore, it is particularly important that the EU focus on strengthening individual responsibility in any future Eurozone reforms.

IV. THE THREAT TO THE PRIVATE SPHERE

As a result of increasing digitalization of the economy, the protection of the private sphere and of personal data is becoming increasingly difficult. What are the consequences? If people value the protection of their private sphere, the threat to this private sphere is also a threat to the common good.

But the consequences are more widespread. If it is possible to screen people more and more thoroughly, certain insurance markets might in future function less effectively, for example health insurance. For instance, if genetic testing can show that certain people are at high risk of a hereditary illness, they will find it very hard to obtain insurance. Companies that have more information about individual customers gain market power and can exploit them. If the state has more opportunities for monitoring citizens, it can extend its tax-related access, or restrict citizens' freedom in other ways. Here the goal should be to prevent abuse without destroying new opportunities that are naturally offered, for example in the realm of digitalization.

V. POPULISM

There is currently much talk about the dangers populism poses to the common good. Populism can be seen as a form of politics that has simple but usually ineffective or even counter-productive remedies for solving complex problems. We must nevertheless recognize that it is part of the nature of democratic processes that many voters are convinced time and again by questionable arguments or are driven, when casting their vote, more by gut instinct than by profound political or economic analyses. Donald Trump can certainly be criticized for being a populist in this sense. But was it not also a populist decision suddenly to accelerate Germany's abandonment of nuclear energy after the most recent nuclear accident in Japan, although no comparable risks exist in Germany? The outcome of democratic decision-making processes is not the same as the common good. The common good is protected if we design these decision-making processes in such a way that the damage is limited even if particularly stupid and malicious people gain positions of power.

VI. THE DANGEROUS DESIRE FOR A WORLD GOVERNMENT

Checks and balances that can keep a rein on populists also play a central role in the debate about global governance. The nation-state's possibilities for action are limited. The impression often arises that economics may be globalized but politics is not, and that many of the problems of our age result from this misunderstanding. This is true, and global warming is the best example of this.

Against this backdrop, many people would like to see more opportunities for collective action at an international level, ideally a kind of assertive world government. This desire for a world government is based on the idea that this world government would be wiser than the average among existing national governments. But it is unclear why this might be the case. In light of the necessarily huge distance between such a government and its citizens, the opposite should be the assumption. Advocates of this solution usually do not imagine that major criminals and fraudsters—of which there have been many in history and are still large numbers today—could take control of this world government. We should be grateful that today such a world government has not appeared, and concentrate

on solving global problems through global cooperation, even if this is laborious.

VII. CONCLUSION

Awareness of the importance of the common good
and of threats to it is a good basis on which to protect
the common good in the future as well. "The best
way of predicting the future is to create it," is another
quotation attributed to Willy Brandt. The future is
open. We can consider ourselves lucky to be living in
democratic constitutional states that are of course not
perfect but which nevertheless function well. Among
other things this means that we are invited to create
the future of the common good.

CHAPTER 15

HOW TO STAY HUMAN IN THE AGE OF AI

HANS ULRICH OBRIST, HITO STEYERL, AND MATTEO PASQUINELLI

An edited transcript of a conversation between Hans Ulrich Obrist, Hito Steyerl, and Matteo Pasquinelli at the Convoco 3.0 event "Artificial Intelligence and the Common Good" on April 1, 2017 in Berlin

Hans Ulrich Obrist: Thank you so much to Corinne Flick for bringing us all together again in such an amazing way. I think this idea of always having artists involved in a very central way in conversations about society, technology, and science goes back to two very important and inspiring models from the 1960s. There was, of course, the organization Experiments in Art and Technology founded by Billy Klüver and others, where they brought artists together with engineers for joint creative projects. Then, in London in the 1960s, Barbara Steveni and John Latham of the Artist Placement Group went even further than that by saying that, actually, artists should be active voices in wider society, and that we should have in every company and in every government an artist in residence. So these two moments have been an important inspiration for bringing artists into the mix.

This leads us right away to today's conversation, which is a continuation of a conversation we had with Hito Steyerl in Paris a couple of months ago, when the Google Cultural Institute invited us to talk about art and AI.

Hito and I were there with the architect Rem Koolhaas, the artist Rachel Rose, and several engineers, including Kenric McDowell and also Mike Tyka. Corinne suggested then that it was urgent to involve a philosopher, so we are delighted to have Matteo Pasquinelli with us today. A very warm welcome to Matteo and to Hito.

Hito, I thought we could begin with something you said in Paris that fascinated me a lot. We talked about AI and machine-learning and psychology. You somehow connected Freud to Google's computer vision program Deep Dream.

Hito Steyerl: This was indeed quite interesting, how psychology pops up again in a place where you wouldn't really expect it. This discussion at Google centered around how neural networks find patterns in images. Then it turned out that, actually, no one, including the engineers, knows how this really works. Basically, people are always trying to figure out how are they thinking, how they are really doing what they do. This coalesced into a set of metaphors, which all had to do with the soul, or the unconscious even. I thought it was such an unexpected place for a discourse of psychology, the unconscious, and the soul to re-emerge.

HUO: Matteo, you also talk about psychology. I listened to an online course you gave a couple of months ago, where you talked about the beginnings of cybernetics and how many of the early cyberneticians had a training in psychology.

Matteo Pasquinelli: The first cyberneticians were indeed all trained in cognitive science. It's interesting to note that the first successful model of artificial intelligence, that is an artificial neural network, was designed to imitate the eye rather than the brain, and in particular the frog's eye. What we have today, basically, is not artificial intelligence as it was imagined in the 1950s, but something different. It's called deep learning, as it involves deep neural networks made up of multiple strata of neurons exactly as in the eye.

HUO: How would you say, then, that art connects to all of this? Earlier today we heard about induction and deduction, and I think you wanted to add something to that.

MP: David Dindi gave a great presentation of this problem.[1] He managed to describe the foundational problems of the paradigm of artificial intelligence. But there is also a third logic category, which is the category of abduction. So you have induction, deduction, and abduction. Abduction is what any poet or artist does when they invent a new metaphor. For instance, we have the expression "the leg of the table." It's very difficult to teach a machine this expression. But we are able to understand it immediately thanks to a similarity between two different domains, the domain of furniture and the domain of animals or human beings with a leg. The metaphoric power of the human being—and of the artist in particular—is something which is very difficult to automatize. That's one of the limits of artificial intelligence: you can automatize a low-skilled lawyer, but a highly qualified lawyer is very difficult to automatize, because a good lawyer is able to invent a new metaphor, a new strategy, to get round a legal obstacle.

HUO: Hito, do you want to comment on that?

HS: Sometimes the research itself produces amazing metaphors. Let me briefly describe the work I'm doing now. I was very privileged lately to shoot documentary footage with a company based in Cambridge that has a very ambitious artificial intelligence project. They want to create a taxonomy of every sound in the world. Image recognition has made huge strides in the past decades, but sound recognition is apparently still in its infancy. They are trying to teach some kind of AI how to recognize sounds. How do they do that? It's really amazing.

The first sound they taught the machine to recognize was the sound of breaking windows. Literally, for weeks on end they went to an old airplane hangar to break hundreds and thousands of windows. They did it themselves. It's not like they were employing construction workers. The engineers went and broke windows. I was totally fascinated with that. They said: this was the production of knowledge; we are working at the cutting edge of the production of knowledge. It's true. Now, of course, why are they breaking windows? Because the AI they are teaching is a smart home appliance, meaning that if someone tries to break into your home, then a machine will pick this up and call the police or riot squad or SWAT team, or something like that. So this sound recognition already has an application in security.

As I was thinking about this, I remembered that there was a very influential social theory in the 1980s, which was called the "broken windows theory." It said, basically, that in any area of a city where only one window was broken and left unrepaired, social decrepitude would immediately set in. There would be drugs, crime, and violence. House prices would go down. There would be social segregation. Thus, a whole methodology of policing was invented, which was called "zero tolerance" policing. No window could be broken.

So what I'm asking myself now is: what is the state of society when, basically, you have to break all the windows. What is a broken windows society as a sort of pinnacle of science? What does it mean if suddenly all the windows have to be broken? What is the social effect of this? Then I thought maybe there is already a prototype for this. I don't know if you've been to London in the past few years, but there is already a very iconic building that basically embodies this. That is The Shard.

The Shard is a very tall building in London which looks as if it is made from broken glass shards. It's in fact the highest building in the city. I think one could call it a monument to class inequality. That is what The Shard is essentially, because it is mainly empty. It is a place where capital is parked. It is not really used for people to live in, but it is a sort of empty tower of money. I think that the broken windows society that is being anticipated is a society where you have this extreme class inequality, where people in the upper levels of the building look down on the lower levels and see that, basically, they don't have to worry about rising waters due to climate change. Even if in London the water rises to the third floor or so, they will be fine in the upper floors. I think that the model of the broken windows society as it stands is basically condensed—to come back to Freud and the metaphor—in this kind of urban architecture.

MP: The broken windows theory is a good example also of problems that, for instance, even the New York Police Department (NYPD) recognizes today, namely, the ethnic and racial bias of the algorithms used in artificial intelligence. The NYPD recently organized a conference about the predictive algorithm that it's now using, which automatizes the broken windows theory and applies that to the map of New York, amplifying social and racial stereotypes. It was realized that—surprise!—the ghettos that were already black on their map were getting blacker and poorer.

It's interesting to note today that this strange amplification of norms also existed in the past. I think that today the algorithms of artificial intelligence are just amplifying established norms. And we see also that they migrate to more sophisticated datascapes. The problem the NYPD had with predictive algorithms also occurred in Afghanistan and Yemen, where the US National Security Agency's system Skynet was used to target potential terrorists, but then killed innocent civilians. I can see that artificial intelligence is expanding social bias at a global level.

HUO: So far we have talked about AI and about machine-learning, but there is also AS or artificial stupidity. Hito, you talk a lot about AS.

HS: Yes, let me connect the dots. If you combine AI with Moore's Law, the law that computing power grows at an exponential rate, then you would expect that AI will eventually catch up with and even surpass human intelligence. But there is one law which is even more important than Moore's Law. It's the most important scientific law ever. It's called Murphy's Law. There is a long version: You have a slice of bread which is buttered, you drop it, and there is a probability of 100 percent that it will land on the buttered side. Please try it. You cannot go wrong with it. It's experimentally proven this will happen.

The short version of Murphy's Law is this: whatever can go wrong, will go wrong. I think this is a very important thing to remember also in artificial intelligence, where people tend to say, oh, this cannot happen, because you just pull the plug. Something will happen, most definitely. I think in the case of AI this has already happened. The first time I was even considering anything like this was a couple of years ago when I came across a Twitter bot called hakan750048, or something like that.

Why did I come across this specific Twitter bot? He was part of a bot army deployed by Turkish President Erdoğan's AKP Party in order to influence the elections in Turkey two years ago or so, I think. This was, and still is, a very popular tool in elections to try to sway public opinion and to deflect popular hashtags. I said to myself, this is artificial intelligence, but very low grade. It's really just two lines of script, or maybe five. It's nothing very sophisticated at all. Yet the social implications of these kinds of artificial stupidities, as I call them, are already monumental in global politics.

Any time I see a vending machine for tickets I feel like this is the singularity staring at me. First of all, I cannot operate these things. I want to buy a ticket. It never works. I'm always getting rejected by it. The way in which automation has already interfered in societies—all the speakers have talked about it today—is not to be underestimated. In that sense, I think the singularity is here already. It is here in the sense of artificial stupidity, which is surrounding us and has already managed to change societies.

HUO: Matteo, what's your take on AS?

MP: We design machine intelligence to start as an ignorant system that grows by learning and becomes less ignorant. The model that we call "good old-fashioned artificial intelligence" failed. This is the idea of automatizing human logic as in Leibniz, in Babbage, in Turing, and in Marvin Minsky. Neural networks are not an imitation of human logic, but of the structure of the human brain. You have a kind of machine, which starts like a blank slate, or like a kid without knowledge, and you have to train this machine, as you do with a kid. These machines are effective because they are ignorant: they know that they are not "intelligent." They possess a kind of designed ignorance that is eager to learn. What matters is the way they grow and learn, that is the information you feed them.

HUO: One thing which, in relation to that, comes to my mind is something we also spoke about this week with Ben Vickers, the artist and Chief Technology Officer at the Serpentine Galleries in London. It's something, Hito, you wrote about, which is of course deeply connected to AI and the common good, namely, the topic of proxy politics. I think it's very critical to the discussion. You describe proxies as devices or scripts tasked with getting rid of noise as well as the bot army hell-bent on producing it. Can you tell us a little bit more about your idea of proxy politics?

HS: The proxy is a fascinating concept, because it characterizes on different levels—political, but also technological—the way the world seems to be organized in many ways right now. Things are done via proxy. They are not done directly, but there are delegates. Things are being outsourced. They are basically handed on to what could, for example, be proxy armies in the biggest and longest ongoing war, the one in Syria, which is a huge proxy army mess where, basically, a sort of Third World War is going on. It's mostly fought by way of proxies.

If you look at how communication is done on the Internet, then this is also on many different technological levels being done by proxies, down to the level of the individual user or consumer, who communicates by way of other tasks. We could bring in the whole topic of trolls, for example, who are basically their own proxies or someone else's proxies, and so on.

HUO: Matteo, what is your take on proxy politics? You showed me earlier today your still confidential but soon to be released scheme, which kind of explains the world. It would be good to hear a little bit from you about proxy politics and how it's been written into your scheme.

MP: You are referring to the syllabus I'm teaching next summer semester at the Karlsruhe University of Arts and Design. We are covering proxy politics as the issue of operational images in warfare. It's interesting how the army, especially in the US, has been investing in artificial intelligence from the beginning. As we know, the development of new technologies is often driven by the army. Harun Farocki was one of the first artists to investigate this relationship between the synthetic image produced by intelligent weapons, the weaponization of images, and the construction of a new visual landscape via military technologies.

Farocki introduced this idea of "operational image" referring to the automation of vision, a technique pioneered during the First Gulf War. That's a good example of a proxy relation. Artificial intelligence, when it plays a role in facial recognition, as shown by the works of the late Farocki, is a good example of the convergence of industrial production and military infrastructure.

HUO: We should maybe address the topic of war in relation to AI in more depth. The military-industrial complex is potentially a very problematic area of application for AI. Hito, your work has a lot to do with this. You actually went into war zones recently for research.

HS: Yes, but I also went to something which is even more directly relevant to the topic, which is the Robotics Olympics. I don't know whether you've heard about it, but it's basically a competition for companies. They are not tied to the military-industrial complex, but still they test their more or less autonomous bipeds and all sorts of other ped robots against one another. It's very interesting, because as a complete lay person, I tend to think, oh my God, these things are moving, and there will be killer robots any time soon. Actually, the speed at which they move is still very slow. It's glacial. They have to speed up all the recordings of the Robotics Olympics, because it's so boring you can't watch it in action.

Any time one of the robots falls over everyone cheers, because finally something is happening. So this high-end killer robot application may be a little bit down the line. It's not imminent in my view. But what do I know? I just see what is being shown in public. I think the more hidden applications and also the more low-tech ones are way more worrying in the sense of skimming social media, such as making psychograms of different regions that enable people to "predict" the outbreak of uprisings. That's more likely.

MP: I would like just to add something to this: what's happening on literally the other side of the weapon and how, indeed, this new form of machine intelligence is changing us and our lives. It's interesting to note that, paradoxically, the poorest countries are developing the first and strongest experience of machine intelligence in these kind of proxy wars. In some regions of Afghanistan and Yemen, inhabitants know that if they deviate in a strange way from their path when they commute from one village to another, that is, if they produce an anomaly in their daily routines, they can be detected as suspicious persons by drones.

This shows how they are already embodying a counter-algorithmic behavior. It's not happening to those who live in Berlin, for instance, even if we can sense the influence of algorithms through our smartphones, for example. It's important to be reminded of the tragic destinies of people who are on the other side of the most sophisticated machine intelligence systems used by the army. Of course, this is happening precisely because these algorithms are not very accurate. The Skynet scandal showed that in many cases civilians were killed because they were mistaken by the algorithm for a group of terrorists.

The enemy is constructed computationally today, but algorithms often miscalculate. There are many other stories to tell about this, but what's striking for me is how these people are already embodying a counter-algorithmic behavior in their daily lives, so as to not be detected as anomalies in the database of some algorithm.

HUO: I have a last question, because I'm aware that we are running out of time. When we spoke with Corinne about this panel, we talked about this idea of the visible and the invisible, knowing that, actually, many of the things related to machine-learning and to AI, are, of course, somehow invisible. I wrote a text last week about Etel Adnan and Paul Klee. In the process, I came across, again, both of them independently of each other talking about this idea of art making the invisible visible. I was wondering, maybe Hito first, and then also Matteo, if you could talk a little bit about that.

How can visual arts address or critique AI or machine-learning and its social implication, given, actually, that it's based on algorithms that operate invisibly in the background? That's particularly interesting, of course, in relation to your work, Hito, because it often deals in the effect of visibility. Now most of the pieces of code and software that are deployed in relation to machine-learning remain not only invisible, but inaccessible, within the systems we use on a daily basis. They are there, but they are somehow invisible and inaccessible.

HS: It's very interesting, because I'm a documentary filmmaker by profession, and I realize that during the course of my practice, with the development of the digital, the image itself became invisible, or intangible, or, in a way, removed from human senses, because it's coded as some kind of numbers. If there is no translation device, I don't even know what it is. My source material is removed from my senses. That's an interesting thing to start with.

The thing that always somehow remains tangible, or within the grasp of human intelligibility, is the narrative around certain technologies, because they are always being told in the form of stories, anecdotes, narratives, and also metaphors. We were talking about social effects. How do technologies relate to the changing of political social systems? If you go into narrative, you can still grasp some kind of logic. Going back to Freud and the unconscious, it's almost like a dream analysis.

We were talking last time about how strange it is that many of these technologies are prefaced by the word "deep." Why is it that they are called "deep mind," "deep dream," "deep neural networks"? This is the question I'm asking myself. Is the corresponding political paradigm one of the "deep state"? How do we read metaphor? How do we decode the narratives in which the technology is transmitted to us?

MP: Next semester I start my course at the Karlsruhe University of Arts and Design with Paul Klee who, in his notebooks, was proposing this idea of the thinking eye, or of visual thinking. From that, I try to cross the 20th century and translate this universe over to machine intelligence, which is conflating the visual form and the thinking form into one thing. To understand what artificial intelligence is, one has to realize to what degree that "intelligence" is still influenced by a visual paradigm.

Warren McCulloch and Walter Pitts, when they conceived the first artificial neural network, were imitating the anatomy of the retina. In fact they were trying to develop a machine to automate pattern recognition. That's something very important to remember for any visual artist. Then one day, the database describing visual inputs was replaced with a database of social data. The eye that was used to detect visual patterns then was used in the same way as an algorithm to detect social patterns. It's interesting for me how you find a visual paradigm within the very technology of artificial intelligence.

HUO: That could not be a better conclusion. Now it's the moment to open it up to the audience. We have time for two or three questions.

Audience member: I have a question concerning what we can learn from the art world, because I think the biggest difference between an artist and a programmer is that the artist is constantly being confronted with what people interpret in her art, and so she always has to explain herself. Or at least the artist's process is a conscious process of constantly asking "what am I doing here?" When you look at programmers, they usually create a world, which is shaping our world, and it brings bias.

To provide an example: I work for a tech company. It showed me its newest facial recognition software. The software didn't recognize me.

All it was supposed to do was tell me I'm female, but it didn't recognize me back then because my complexion didn't really match the pictures usually fed into the machine, because I was wearing less makeup and more clothing. Usually programmers are not confronted with their biases. I always think it's really interesting how in art you debate where you're coming from. How can we transmit that discussion into that other community?

HS: It's fascinating, absolutely. If I do just anything, say a doodle, I have to take responsibility for that. People will yell at me and what not. But whatever I do, doesn't change anything. It's completely inconsequential. If people design programmes for facial recognition, by contrast, the consequences are significant, but I don't think there is any kind of visual literacy debate going on around it. What is being represented? How is it being done? How do you come to this conclusion? I'm thinking of this study, which actually does not really have a viable application, by Chinese researchers, who have developed some contraption to "identify" criminals by the way they look.

The ones who are less attractive tend to be more criminal according to them. What kind of idea of image, of the visual, of aesthetics, of its relation to society and so on, is condensed in this kind of technology? That would be really interesting to question from an artistic point of view.

It's effectively like phrenology, which was around in the 19th century. Phrenology is a method based on the form of skulls and theories of superiority. Basically, the same thing is now re-emerging through AI. This is a bit threatening.

MP: Supervised machine-learning is when you tell a machine to review patterns that you know already. Then there are other forms of machine-learning that are unsupervised, such as when you give a database to a machine, and you just let the machine improvise and make things emerge. That's, of course, a new domain. We are familiar with Google's Deep Dream algorithm and all these crazy, trippy, psychedelic faces that emerge, for example when applying facial recognition of dogs and cats to a completely random image.

There is also a new strategy that we are starting to explore thanks to some programmers, where what we do is abnormalize. We don't let a predictable pattern emerge, but we explore different, new norms that could be used for the visual landscape, but also for the database of social relations. This is important for art and for the history of perspective as well, because this, indeed, is a new perspective on the world, on society.

During the Renaissance, with the help of simple geometric rules, a new vision of the city was produced at a time that also saw significant developments in architecture. Today we are opening up new datascapes, new visions, so to speak, that were not possible 50 years ago, or even ten years ago.

HUO: We can take one more question.

Audience member: I would like to have your take on the notion that a lot of the anxiety that people have is a product of the conflation of consciousness, or artificial consciousness, with artificial intelligence, and how that relates to how you define what art is. What is a product of a computer, or an AI producing a piece of art versus a human, and how can we differentiate between the two?

MP: In my opinion, machines are not conscious, but of course they contribute to an unconscious. Walter Benjamin famously introduced the idea of the "optical unconscious" that is produced by photography. We can work in an optical medium. We can discuss that. Then, of course, the machine is producing a new form of non-conscious cognition, or non-conscious visual landscape. This is also the important example of machine vision and the work of Harun Farocki on the "operational image." Images are produced by machines for other machines. That's something that's happening in terms of the image regime beyond our sight.

In the same way, you can even hypothesize the production and transmission of concepts from machine to machine that are happening outside of the engagement of our brains. That's a way to frame the issue of consciousness. I believe that machines are not conscious. We must not make the mistake of anthropomorphizing machines, so we cannot use terms that we use to describe the human mind to describe other things.

HS: For me, it doesn't really matter. My point is, OK, maybe future AIs will be conscious or maybe not. They will certainly be intelligent. That's all fair and fine. The point is that there are so many existing phenomena already that I think we need to deal with those that are being caused by the by-products of all these technological developments. I think that this is where people should focus their attention, because if you're just always in awe of the next new thing coming, either benevolent or an obnoxious singularity, then you will fail to recognize that our societies now are already being restructured in a way that enables post-fascism, nativism, populism, unemployment, and all of these things. That's my point.

Fantastic research is being done on trying to detect signals from alien intelligence. Huge radio telescopes are being built. I think it's really beautiful and fascinating, but wouldn't it be even better to have the same kind of observatory to detect human intelligence? I think this is much more important.

HUO: That is a wonderful conclusion. Thank you so, so much Hito and Matteo.

Note

1. At the Convoco 3.0 event on April 1, 2017 in Berlin, David Dindi gave a talk about how combining human inductive reasoning and artificial deductive reasoning will result in collective intelligence, a hybrid intelligence that will draw upon both strengths to move us towards encompassing infinite knowledge.

CONTRIBUTORS

Prof. Dr. h.c. Roland Berger is the Founder and since 2010 Honorary Chairman of Roland Berger GmbH in Munich. With 50 offices in 36 countries and 2,400 employees, today the company is one of the world's top five biggest strategy consultants, and advises leading international companies in the industrial and service sectors, as well as public institutions. Prof. Dr. Berger is a member of many national and international advisory committees and supervisory boards, foundations, and organizations. He has also been appointed to numerous committees of experts in the EU Commission, federal and state governments.

Roland Berger is Chairman of the Board of Trustees of the Roland Berger Foundation, which he founded. The Foundation is dedicated to the global protection of human dignity and human rights, and throughout Germany it supports gifted and dedicated children and young people from socially disadvantaged families in their education from primary school to their school-leaving examinations. Since 2015 the Foundation has also worked with unaccompanied minors in Germany.

Univ. Prof. em. Dr. sc. tc. hc. Bazon Brock, thinker-at-large and artist without portfolio, is Emeritus Professor of Aesthetics and Cultural Education at the Bergische Universität in Wuppertal, Germany; in 2016 he was awarded the Von der Heydt Prize by the City of Wuppertal. Previous professorships include those at Hamburg University of Fine Arts (1965–76) and the University of Applied Arts, Vienna (1977–80). In 1992 he was awarded an honorary doctorate at ETH (Swiss Federal Institute for Technology, Zürich) and in 2012 at the Hochschule für Gestaltung, Karlsruhe. Since 2014 he has been Honorary Professor for Prophecy at HBKsaar (Saar College of Fine Arts), Saarbrücken. He has developed the method of "Action Teaching," in which the seminar hall becomes a place of enactment, for oneself and others. Between 1968 and 1992 he led the documenta schools for visitors, which he founded in Kassel. From 2010 to 2013 he ran courses for "professional citizens" at the Karlsruhe University of Arts and Design. He has organized around 3,000 events and "action plays," most recently *Lustmarsch durchs Theoriegelände* (2006, in eleven museums). He is a member of the Institut für theoretische Kunst, Universalpoesie und Prognostik and Founder of the Amt für Arbeit an unlösbaren Problemen und Maßnahmen der hohen Hand, Berlin (www.denkerei-berlin.de).

Prof. Dr. Dr. Udo Di Fabio began his professional career in Dinslaken, North Rhine-Westphalia in 1970 as a middle-grade municipal administrator. During this time he went back to school to complete his high school graduation, subsequently studying jurisprudence at Ruhr-Universität Bochum and the social sciences at Duisburg University (today the University of Duisburg-Essen).

After passing state examinations in law in 1982 and 1985, Prof. Dr. Dr. Udo Di Fabio worked initially as a Judge at the Duisburg Court of Social Welfare, before, in 1986, becoming a Research Assistant at the Institute of Public Law at the University of Bonn. He completed his doctoral thesis there one year later, and in 1990 he wrote a doctoral thesis in the social sciences. In 1993, after completing his postdoctoral research, he was appointed Professor of Public Law at the University of Münster, and a few months later he accepted an appointment at the University of Trier. Between 1997 and 2003 Prof. Dr. Dr. Udo Di Fabio taught at Ludwig-Maximilian University Munich. Since 2003 he has been Professor of Public Law at the University of Bonn.

On December 16, 1999 Prof. Dr. Dr. Udo Di Fabio was appointed Justice of the Second Senate in Germany's Federal Constitutional Court. His department covered in particular European law, international law, and parliamentary law. On December 19, 2011, at the end of his twelve-year term of office, he received the Grand Cross of the Order of Merit of the Federal Republic of Germany. His publications include contributions as Co-Editor of the academic journal *Archiv des öffentlichen Rechts*.

Dr. Corinne Michaela Flick studied both law and literature, taking American studies as her subsidiary, at Ludwig-Maximilian University Munich. She gained her Dr. Phil. in 1989. She has worked as in-house lawyer for Bertelsmann Buch AG and Amazon.com. In 1998, she became General Partner in Vivil GmbH und Co. KG, Offenburg. She is Founder and Chair of the Convoco Foundation. As Editor of Convoco! Editions she has published the following volumes:

Authority in Transformation (Convoco! Editions, 2017); *Power and its Paradoxes* (Convoco! Editions, 2016); *To Do or Not To Do—Inaction as a Form of Action* (Convoco! Editions, 2015); *Dealing with Downturns: Strategies in Uncertain Times* (Convoco! Editions, 2014); *Collective Lawbreaking—A Threat to Liberty* (Convoco! Editions, 2013); *Who Owns the World's Knowledge?* (Convoco! Editions, 2012); *Staatsfinanzierung und Wirtschaftsfinanzierung am Scheideweg* (FVA, 2010); *Das demographische Problem als Gefahr für Rechtskultur und Wirtschaft* (FVA, 2009).

Dr. Carl Benedikt Frey is Co-Director of the Oxford Martin Programme on Technology and Employment at the Oxford Martin School, and Economics Associate of Nuffield College, both University of Oxford. He is also a Senior Fellow of the Programme on Employment, Equity and Growth at the Institute for New Economic Thinking in Oxford, and the Department of Economic History at Lund University, Sweden. His research focuses on the transition of industrial nations to digital economies, and the subsequent challenges for economic growth, labor markets, and urban development. To secure impact for his research outside academia, Dr. Frey is widely engaged in policy, advisory, and media activities. In partnership with Citigroup, he works to help global leaders navigate the rapidly changing world economy. Over the course of his career, he has also worked with the Swedish Government, among others, and acted as a Specialist Advisor to the Digital Skills Select Committee to the British House of Lords. He has also been an external consultant to various international organizations (e.g. OECD and UN agencies) and leading corporations (e.g. Deloitte and PwC).

Prof. Dr. Clemens Fuest gained his doctorate at the University of Cologne in 1994 and his postdoctoral qualification at Ludwig-Maximilian University Munich in 2001, when he was appointed Professor of Political Economy at the University of Cologne, until 2008, and Visiting Professor at Bocconi University in Milan. From 2008 to 2013 he was Professor of Business Taxation and Research Director of the University of Oxford Centre for Business Taxation. Between 2013 and 2015 he was President and Director of Science and Research of the Centre for European Economic Research (ZEW) and Professor of Economics at the University of Mannheim. Since 2016 he has been President of the Ifo Institute for Economic Research in Munich.

Clemens Fuest has been a member of the Academic Advisory Board of the German Federal Ministry of

Finance since 2003 and Head of the Board 2007–10. From 2012 to 2014 he was a member of the Advisory Board for Sustainable Development of the state government of Baden-Württemberg. He was a member of The Market Economy Foundation's scientific council Kronberger Kreis 2004–08, and again from 2013. Since 2014 he has been a member of the EU High-level Group on Own Resources, and since 2015 a member of the Germany's Minimum Wage Commission. He is Programme Director of the University of Oxford Centre for Business Taxation, a member of numerous German and international scientific academies and associations, and is on the board of the International Institute for Public Finance. He serves on the editorial boards of several scientific journals and is editor of *Beiträge zur Finanzwissenschaft* (Contributions to Financial Research).

Prof. Dr. Kai A. Konrad is Director at the Max Planck Institute for Tax Law and Public Finance and a Scientific Member of the Max Planck Society. He was a Full Professor of Economics at the Freie Universität Berlin from 1994 to 2009, and from 2001 to 2009 he was a Director at the Wissenschaftszentrum Berlin für Sozialforschung (WZB). He is a member of the German National Academy of Sciences Leopoldina and of four other science academies. He is a Co-editor of the *Journal of Public Economics*. Since 1999 he has been a member of the Council of Scientific Advisors to the Federal Ministry of Finance and was the Chair from 2011 to 2014.

Prof. Dr. Stefan Korioth gained his doctorate in law in 1990 and completed his postdoctoral qualification in public and constitutional law. From 1996 to 2000 he was Professor of Public Law, Constitutional History, and Theory of Government at Greifswald. In 2000 he accepted the Chair of Public and Ecclesiastical Law at Ludwig-Maximilian University Munich. His publications include *Integration und Bundesstaat* (1990), *Der Finanzausgleich zwischen Bund und Ländern* (1997), *Grundzüge des Staatskirchenrechts* (with B. Jean d'Heur, 2000), and *Das Bundesverfassungsgericht* (with Klaus Schlaich, 9th edition, 2012).

Prof. Dr. h.c. Rudolf Mellinghoff is President of the Federal Fiscal Court. He studied at the University of Münster and served his postgraduate legal internship in Baden-Württemberg. Between 1984 and 1987 he was a Research Assistant at the University of Heidelberg, becoming a Judge in the Finance Court of Düsseldorf in 1987. From 1987 to 1991 he was a Research Fellow at the Federal Constitutional Court. He was appointed Judge at the Finance Court of Düsseldorf in 1989. Prof. Dr. h.c. Mellinghoff was Head of Department at the Ministry of Justice of Mecklenburg-Vorpommern between July 1991 and June 1992, and was appointed Presiding Judge of the Finance Court in 1996. In a second full-time position, he served as Judge of the Higher Administrative Court of Mecklenburg-Vorpommern between 1992 and 1996. From 1995 to 1996 he was also a member of the Constitutional Court of Mecklenburg-Vorpommern, and from 1997 to 2001 served as Judge at the Federal Supreme Finance Court. From January 2001 to October 2011, Prof. Dr. h.c. Mellinghof served as Justice in the Second Senate of the Federal Constitutional Court. Since then he has been President of the Federal Supreme Court of Finance. In 2006 Rudolf Mellinghoff was awarded an Honorary Doctorate from the University of Greifswald, and in 2007 from the Eberhard Karls University in Tübingen. In 2011 he was awarded the Grand Merit Cross with Star and Sash of the Order of Merit of the Federal Republic of Germany. He is currently Chair both of the Deutsche Steuerjuristische Gesellschaft and of the Advisory Council of the Berliner Steuergespräche e.V. He is a member of the Judicial Integrity Group, and from 2009 to 2011 was President of the German

Section of the International Commission of Jurists, becoming Vice-President in 2012.

Prof. Dr. Timo Meynhardt holds the Dr. Arendt Oetker Chair of Business Psychology and Leadership at the HHL Leipzig Graduate School of Management. He is Managing Director of the Center for Leadership and Values in Society at the University of St. Gallen, where he obtained his doctorate and post-doctoral qualification in business administration. For several years, he was Practice Expert at McKinsey & Company.

Prof. Dr. Meynhardt's work focuses on public value management, leadership and competency diagnostics, combining psychology and businesss management in his research and teaching. He publishes the *Public Value Atlas* for Switzerland and Germany, which aims at making transparent the social benefits of companies and organizations (www.gemeinwohlatlas.de, www.gemeinwohl.ch). His Public Value Scorecard provides a management tool to measure and analyze the creation of public value. He is also Patron of the EY Public Value Awards for Startups (www.eypva.com).

Hans Ulrich Obrist is Co-Director of the Serpentine Galleries, London. Prior to this, he was curator of the Musée d'Art Moderne de la Ville, Paris. Since his first show *World Soup (The Kitchen Show)* in 1991, he has curated more than 250 exhibitions. In 2009 Obrist was made Honorary Fellow of the Royal Institute of British Architects (RIBA), and in 2011 received the CCS Bard Award for Curatorial Excellence. Hans Ulrich Obrist has lectured internationally at academic and art institutions, and is contributing editor to several magazines and journals.

His recent publications include *A Brief History of Curating* (2008), *Everything You Always Wanted to Know About Curating But Were Afraid to Ask* (2011), *Do It: The Compendium* (2013), *Think Like Clouds* (2014), *Ai Weiwei Speaks* (2016), *Ways of Curating* (2015), and a new volume in his *Conversation Series*.

Dr. Stefan Oschmann has been Chairman of the Executive Board and CEO of Merck since 2016. Prior to that he served as Vice-Chairman and Deputy CEO, with responsibility for group strategy, among other things. He joined Merck in 2011 as a member of the Executive Board and was responsible for the healthcare business sector until the end of 2014. He drove the transformation of biopharma business and played an instrumental role in the group-wide transformation and growth program "Fit for 2018." Before joining Merck, Stefan Oschmann worked for the US pharma company MSD. He started his career at an agency of the United Nations, and also worked for the German Chemical Industry Association (VCI). He holds a doctorate in veterinary medicine from Ludwig-Maximilian University Munich.

Prof. Dr. Matteo Pasquinelli who holds a Masters from the University of Bologna and a PhD from the University of London, is a philosopher and Professor of Media Theory at the University of Arts and Design, Karlsruhe. He also recently taught at the Pratt Institute in New York. He is the author of *Animal Spirits: A Bestiary of the Commons* (2008), and editor of *Gli algoritmi del capitale* (2014) and *Alleys of Your Mind: Augmented Intelligence and Its Traumas* (2015). He teaches regularly at universities and art institutions on the interface between political philosophy, media theory, and cognitive science, and publishes frequently in academic journals and art publications. In 2014, he co-curated the exhibition *The Ultimate Capital is the Sun* and the symposium *The Metabolism of the Social Brain* at the Neue Gesellschaft für Bildende Kunst, Berlin and the Berlin University of the Arts.

Prof. Dr. Christoph G. Paulus studied law at Munich, taking his doctorate in law in 1980. His postdoctoral qualification, gained in 1991, was in civil law, civil procedure, and Roman law, for which he was awarded the Medal of the University of Paris II. Between 1989 and 1990, he was a recipient of a Feodor Lynen Stipend from the Humboldt Foundation in Berkeley, from which he had earlier gained his LL.M. From 1992 to 1994 he was Associate Professor at Augsburg, and from the summer semester 1994 he was at the Law Faculty of Humboldt University in Berlin, becoming Dean of the Faculty 2008–10. He is Consultant to the International Monetary Fund and the World Bank. Among other roles, he is a member (and Director) of the International Insolvency Institute of the American College of Bankruptcy and the International Association for Procedural Law. Since 2006 he has been advisor on insolvency law to the German delegation to UNCITRAL. He is on the editorial board of the *Zeitschrift für Wirtschaftsrecht* (ZIP), the *Norton Annual Review of International Insolvency,* and the *International Insolvency Law Review.*

Prof. Jörg Rocholl is President of ESMT European School of Management and Technology in Berlin and holds the Ernst & Young Chair in Governance and Compliance. He studied economic sciences at the Universität Witten/Herdecke, where he earned a degree in economics (with honors) in 1999. After completing his Ph.D. at Columbia University in New York, he was appointed an Assistant Professor at the University of North Carolina at Chapel Hill. Prof. Rocholl has researched and taught at ESMT since 2007, being appointed its President in 2011. He is a member of the Economic Advisory Board of the German Federal Ministry of Finance, Research Professor at the Ifo Institute for Economic Research in Munich, and Duisenberg Fellow of the European Central Bank (ECB).

Prof. Dr. Dr. h.c. Wolfgang Schön was awarded his doctorate of law at the University of Bonn in 1985, and in 1992 he received his postdoctoral qualification there. He was Professor at the University of Bielefeld from 1992 to 1996, and from 1996 to 2002 was again at Bonn. Since 2002 he has been Director and Scientific Member of the Max Planck Institute for Intellectual Property, Competition, and Tax Law in Munich. He is Honorary Professor at Ludwig-Maximilian University Munich; member of the Global Law Faculty, New York University; and International Research Fellow, University of Oxford Centre of Business Taxation. From 2008 to 2014 Prof. Schön was Vice-President of the Max Planck Society. Since 2014 he has been

Vice-President of the German Research Foundation (DFG). He has published numerous works on company law, competition law, and tax law.

Jens Spahn MdB is a banker and political scientist. Born in Ahaus, North Rhein-Westphalia in 1980, he was elected to the German Bundestag for the first time in 2002 for the constituency of Steinfurt I/Borken I. Between 2009 and 2015 he was Health Spokesman for the CDU/CSU group in the Bundestag, and since July 3, 2015 he has been Parliamentary State Secretary in the Federal Ministry of Finance.

In 1995 Spahn joined the Junge Union Deutschland, and in 1997 the Christian Democratic Union of Germany (CDU). He has been Chairman of the Borken District CDU since 2005, a member of the CDU National Committee since 2012, and in 2014 was elected CDU President at the party conference in Cologne. As Chairman of the German-Dutch Parliamentary Friendship Group he encourages a good cross-border relationship. He has edited two books, *Ins Offene – Deutschland, Europa und die Flüchtlinge* (2015) and, in collaboration with two doctors, *App vom Arzt – Bessere Gesundheit durch digitale Medizin* (2016).

Prof. Dr. Phil. Hito Steyerl is Professor of Experimental Film and Video and the Co-founder of the Research Center for Proxy Politics at the Berlin University of the Arts. She studied cinematography and documentary film in Tokyo and Munich, and wrote her doctoral thesis in philosophy at the Academy of Fine Arts in Vienna. Her research focuses on media, technology, and the distribution of images. In her texts, performances, and essayist documentary films, Prof. Dr. Steyerl deals with postcolonial criticism and the feminist criticism of representational logic. She works at the interface between visual art and film as well as theory and practice. Her numerous works have been exhibited at the Venice Biennale, the Museum of Contemporary Art, Los Angeles and the Museum of Modern Art, New York, among other venues. In addition to her work as an artist, she was a Lecturer at the Centre for Cultural Studies at Goldsmiths College, University of London and was Visiting Professor at the Royal Academy of Copenhagen and the Academy of Fine Arts, Helsinki. In 2016, the Royal College of Art in London awarded her an honorary doctorate. In November 2017, the British art magazine *ArtReview* ranked Hito Steyerl top of their "Power 100" list, as the most influential person in the international art world.

AUTHORITY IN TRANSFORMATION
2017

ISBN: 978-0-9931953-4-1

With contributions by: Claudia Buch, Clemens Fuest, Thomas Hoeren, Peter M. Huber, Kai A. Konrad, Stefan Korioth, Peter Maurer, Hans Ulrich Obrist and Richard Wentworth, Stefan Oschmann, Christoph G. Paulus, Roger Scruton, Wolfgang Schön

POWER AND ITS PARADOXES
2016

ISBN: 978-0-9931953-2-7

With contributions by: Clemens Fuest, Thomas Hoeren, Wolfgang Ischinger, Stefan Korioth, Hans Ulrich Obrist and Simon Denny, Christoph G. Paulus, Albrecht Ritschl, Jörg Rocholl, Roger Scruton, Brendan Simms

TO DO OR NOT TO DO—INACTION AS A FORM OF ACTION
2015

ISBN: 978-0-9931953-0-3

With contributions by: Bazon Brock, Gert-Rudolf Flick, Peter M. Huber, Kai A. Konrad, Stefan Korioth, Friedhelm Mennekes, Hans Ulrich Obrist and Marina Abramović, Christoph G. Paulus, Jörg Rocholl, Wolfgang Schön, Roger Scruton, Pirmin Stekeler-Weithofer

DEALING WITH DOWNTURNS: STRATEGIES IN UNCERTAIN TIMES
2014

ISBN: 978-0-9572958-8-9

With contributions by: Jens Beckert, Bazon Brock, Saul David, Gerd Gigerenzer, Paul Kirchhof, Kai A. Konrad, Stefan Korioth, Christoph G. Paulus, Jörg Rocholl, Burkhard Schwenker

COLLECTIVE LAW-BREAKING—A THREAT TO LIBERTY
2013

ISBN: 978-0-9572958-5-8

With contributions by: Shaukat Aziz, Roland Berger, Christoph G. Paulus, Ingolf Pernice, Wolfgang Schön, Hannes Siegrist, Jürgen Stark, Pirmin Stekeler-Weithofer

WHO OWNS THE WORLD'S KNOWLEDGE?
2012

ISBN: 978-0-9572958-0-3

With contributions by: Eckhard Cordes, Urs Gasser, Thomas Hoeren, Viktor Mayer-Schönberger, Christoph G. Paulus, Jürgen Renn, Burkhard Schwenker, Hannes Siegrist

CAN'T PAY, WON'T PAY? SOVEREIGN DEBT AND THE CHALLENGE OF GROWTH IN EUROPE
2011

ISBN: 978-0-9572958-3-4

With contributions by: Roland Berger, Howard Davies, Otmar Issing, Paul Kirchhof, Kai A. Konrad, Stefan Korioth, Christoph G. Paulus, Burkhard Schwenker